# JOURNEY TO FIND THE PERFECT PARTNER FOREVER

Love Doctor Monti
(aka Neil-Monticelli Harley-Rüdd)

Copyright © 2024 by Love Doctor Monti (aka Neil-Monticelli Harley-Rüdd)

Paperback: 978-1-964744-21-6
Hardback: 978-1-964744-23-0
eBook: 978-1-964744-22-3
Library of Congress Control Number: 2024913758

All rights reserved. No part of this publication may be reproduced, distributed, or transmitted in any form or by any electronic or mechanical means, without the prior written permission of the publisher, except in the case of brief quotations embodied in critical reviews and certain other noncommercial uses permitted by copyright law.

Ordering Information:

Prime Seven Media
518 Landmann St.
Tomah City, WI 54660

Printed in the United States of America

"This book is dedicated to "Mi Criss Ting" Müberra, who was my true inspiration and treasured as my shining light."

# LOST LOVE

It has hit me just like a hurricane

How you went and how you came

I could never believe

That you would ever deceive

It is so hurtful now that we are apart

That you actions keep playing tricks on my heart

I don't wish you any pain

But I don't ever wish to see you again

It is easy to forgive

But it is so hard to forget

Let the biggest crime in life is the crime of regret

*Love Doctor Monti (2024)*

# INTRO | Meet Love Doctor Monti

Neil-Monticelli Harley-Rüdd has been giving insights into love and relationships since the age of 13, when he became a self-professed "Love Doctor".

With his focus on good old-fashioned romance and mutual respect, the results have been dynamic. Clearly he provides the medicine to repair broken hearts, and offers singletons renewed hope to find that seemingly elusive special someone for their forever journey to true love.

He has extensively traveled across the globe and handed out relationship advice, which has stretched from Brazil and the Caribbean to as far as Japan in the other direction.

With decades of experience in helping people find a meaningful romance, the Love Doctor has penned his secrets with this 20-chapter self-help book that will help enlighten and educate singletons seeking a fulfilling relationship.

# CONTENTS

Chapter 1 | Ready For Romance?..................................................1

Chapter 2 | Get Rid Of The Ghosts ...............................................9

Chapter 3 | Where To Start Hunting.............................................17

Chapter 4 | Spark A Conversation ...............................................25

Chapter 5 | Fancy Flirting............................................................35

Chapter 6 | Securing Second Dates..............................................45

Chapter 7 | Rose-Tinted Glasses..................................................57

Chapter 8 | Key To Happiness.....................................................67

Chapter 9 | Ladder of Love .........................................................75

Chapter 10 | Think With Your Head, Love With Your Heart......83

Chapter 11 | Avoid Love Triangles...............................................91

Chapter 12 | Never Neglect ........................................................99

Chapter 13 | Stick or Quit?........................................................107

Chapter 14 | Romance Is Not Dead...........................................115

Chapter 15 | How To Hunt For Perfection.................................125

Chapter 16 | Building Foundations For The Future ...................135

Chapter 17 | Unearthing Our Soulmate .....................................143

Chapter 18 | How To Keep Romance Alive................................153

Chapter 19 | Importance Of Intimacy........................................163

Chapter 20 | Happy Ever After ..................................................173

## Chapter 1 | Ready For Romance?

If you are one of those singletons who has sensibly taken a step back from rushing into a new relationship, then usually there's a reason for your hesitation.

Often this reason is about being insecure, which is understandable if you're one of a ridiculously high number of people that has been cheated on.

Maybe you are relatively inexperienced in romance, or fear rejection for some reason.

It can take time until you find yourself ready to give love a chance. For those who suffered from infidelity then trusting again in a fresh relationship is extremely difficult, so naturally there are barriers.

Time is the only healer for those who have suffered as the injured party. They require time to fully deal with this loss, but can move on.

For those who seriously seek someone new for romance, whatever your circumstances and past experience, just ensure that you give any potential love interest the clean canvas that they warrant.

# Chapter 1 | Ready For Romance?

It's no use apportioning any form of blame on the latest possible partner, otherwise the hangups will be with you rather than them. You need to firmly focus on the future.

You certainly don't wish to treat falling in love like a game of snakes and ladders, so don't throw the dice and hope for the right numbers to materialize to progress.

Finding a relationship requires an element of risk-taking and a leap of faith, as you are putting your trust in someone.

You need to make your love life smooth sailing, so don't gamble with your future choice for a romantic partner. Just make logical choices from the very beginning, and ask close friends what their take is on this new love interest.

Many singletons look for an easy life, so consider dating their former partner when their heart has healed from their latest break-up. However, that will only ever be a diluted version of what you previously experienced and shows weakness, as you have clearly failed to learn from your past experience.

Trying to rekindle things with an ex is simply going down the route of a repeat performance of being hurt, so should be avoided.

Time is the only healer as an injured party. You need time to fully deal with this loss, but you can move on when emotionally ready.

Yet if you still possess an aching heart, then this is far from ideal to start a new romance. This would just become a doomed rebound relationship and be a total waste of your time and efforts. That time could be much better spent with someone for you to build memories

# Chapter 1 | Ready For Romance?

together and potentially create a future, rather than going backwards as it is a simpler solution.

Should you have suffered in the past then now is the time to concentrate on your rebuilding mission to repair your heartache.

Don't allow any unfortunate experiences to leave doubts about yourself and your previous relationship, otherwise you'll be wasting time by analyzing everything that was wrong before.

Once you are truly emotionally ready and feel financially secure, these signal the time for you to be able to embrace a long-term loving relationship. Best to be patient until you are ready to date again.

Keep faith in yourself that you can do so much better romantically next time following the last failed relationship. You must begin to feel confident and ready to bounce back onto the dating scene, as then your positive persona will attract the right sort of attention.

In this ever-evolving world of love and romance, you will have most likely considered joining dating apps and websites. Yet these sadly tend to either be full of fake profiles, those on the hunt for meaningless sex, shallow people who wish to punch above their weight as well as those desperately seeking the perfect person but won't compromise on who ticks all the boxes.

If you are ready to move forward, by being able to take care of yourself both emotionally and financially, then it is imperative to find the confidence to flirt with potential suitors.

The quickest way to start flirting is by alerting your closest friends that you wish to be eased back into society to meet singletons in a bid

# Chapter 1 | Ready For Romance?

to find that seemingly elusive someone special.

With any luck some of them will jump at the chance to play matchmaker, so you'll soon find yourself out in a group to enjoy drinks or food with friends.

If you feel good about yourself and are brimming with confidence then these are a sign that you're ready to love someone. These mean that any potential relationship would be based on want or desire rather than being emotionally needy.

There's no living happily ever after for most couples, because they just aren't committed as they only wish to chase fun and frolics. Now is the time to decide whether you are really ready for a meaningful relationship on a long-term basis.

If you aren't quite ready yet to share your life with a partner then instead take up a new hobby, ideally something that involves exercise to release endorphins that will lift your mood and spirits.

The majority of new gym members are likely to have recently come out of a relationship, which means that it should be jam-packed with singletons. This is a great place to potentially meet your next love interest.

You're much better off waiting to find someone worthy of your love and devotion. An exciting relationship will reignite your faith in romance, but building a new and solid relationship can only occur when you are truly emotionally ready.

You can take heart from the fact that change is the only constant in our lives, but should only consider moving forward when you feel

## Chapter 1 | Ready For Romance?

happy. Fortunately love often strikes when you least expect it, especially when you aren't seeking a romance.

But you will need to have the magic of your mojo back again to be able to embark on a meaningful romance, which is all down to motivation. If you show uncertainty about entering a new relationship then you will no doubt have lost your enthusiasm for life — whether it's down to boredom, exhaustion, feeling sorry for yourself, stress or being either overwhelmed or underwhelmed.

It's essential to take the route to getting your groove back and to improve your emotional well-being by seeking something inspirational and positive, such as learning a language or even magic tricks to impress people.

Also consider upgrading your appearance to make you feel more attractive and happier, which will enhance your self confidence for when you get back on the dating scene and improve your social contact. You can start by making the effort to have conversations with those close to you.

Reminiscing about the good times, when you had immense fun, with friends and family can mentally jolt you into wanting to return to creating memories. To be able to concentrate on making memories with someone special is the ultimate dream for many people, especially those with romantic tendencies.

If you have truly lost your mojo then ensure that you avoid alcohol as well as fatty and sugary foods. It's time to treat your body with kindness and concentrate on an improved version of you — so fill

# Chapter 1 | Ready For Romance?

it with plenty of fruit, lean meat and vegetables. Feeling better and looking better is one way to kickstart being ready for a new relationship.

Remarkable romances have always been portrayed as being the most wondrous and amazing experience. Rightly so, because it's the process that makes the love between two people so spectacular.

These powerful yet sugar-coated romances we read about and watch are created solely for entertainment purposes. These are meant to be aspirational, but are not as run-of-the-mill in real life as they are on the big screen. This means so many hopes are dashed.

If you're a hopeless romantic yet single, then the reason you've yet to meet 'the one' is most likely down to overthinking love and relationships. For example, dreaming about meeting someone tall, dark and attractive looking to end your days of being single will remain a dream unless you make the effort to be proactive and do something about it.

It's not complicated, but romance only functions between those in a loving relationship. Initially you need to be bitten by the bug of love and swept off your feet to begin the journey to find the perfect partner forever.

# Chapter 2 | Get Rid Of The Ghosts

Ghosts sound scary to many people. As well as 'ghosts' from the past suddenly reappearing, there's the total opposite of a vanishing trick that in the modern dating world is known as 'ghosting'.

If you are foolish enough to give someone that you once loved a second chance, which will only be a diluted version of what you originally encountered, then that 'ghost' from the past could haunt you for some time when the relationship will ultimately fail once more.

Although it is important to think with your head and love with your heart, you need to consider the fact that an old flame can potentially have a negative impact on any of your future relationships.

Try to establish why this former squeeze has returned into your life. There was emotional and/or physical distance between you, so why the change? Is this normal behavior for either of you to return into the arms of an ex? Have either of you recently experienced any major life events?

If one, or even both, of you is emotionally needy or emotionally

## Chapter 2 | Get Rid Of The Ghosts

vulnerable then obviously rekindling your relationship is going to be rocky and will keep on stalling.

This scenario will become needlessly complicated for a potential forever relationship, which has already crashed before for whatever reason.

A common motivation for an ex to re-establish contact is when they've suffered so badly that they are grieving. You are just their back-up plan as they previously felt safe and secure with you because of your previous precious love.

If they have experienced something traumatic, you need to be fully aware that you're only their temporary fix to fill their void.

Although it would be far easier to just maintain a friendship, because of your history then you are always going to be genuine and caring with bundles of empathy and compassion. However, this can easily be misinterpreted for showing a romantic interest, with compassion turning into passion. Far too often this relationship leads to the two of you giving it another shot.

This is potentially disastrous as the dating phase, especially in the early stages of a romantic relationship, should be light-hearted and fun. Yet you've pressed the fast forward button and therefore bypassed building up all the excitement and thrills of romance.

All solid relationships should comprise love in three stages. Initially to love affectionately, as friends. It's no use being with someone who can't become your very best friend. Then to love romantically, with thoughtful gestures, before organically moving on to love each other

# Chapter 2 | Get Rid Of The Ghosts

sexually with meaningful love making rather than the lust of pure sex.

When former relationships are rekindled the couple tend to have lost their romance, and too often have forgotten why they were ever friends as they are now completely different people. Instead they have thrown themselves together to concentrate on companionship and sex, which fills any void in their respective lives.

This tends to happen to old flames when they have been apart for decades, and therefore they miss out on true friendship and passionate love making.

Only if you both felt that you were originally soulmates and there was a valid reason why you broke up, should you consider giving this potential relationship another whirl. If you stayed in touch as genuine friends, albeit only occasionally, then at least you will have shown mutual respect and not gone totally off the grid.

At the end of the day self-care and self-esteem are essential. If this possible partnership is the real deal in both of your eyes, then plan a happy future by hitting the reset button. But don't forget to reintroduce the romantic elements.

If you are emotionally and mentally ready to embark on a new romantic relationship, it's vital to put to bed all the 'ghosts' of exes. Avoid where you have been with them before, whether it is a bar, restaurant or even a foreign country.

It's essential to erase memories from your past in order to concentrate and focus on a new you. It is akin to being reborn, so never allow an ex to enter your mind nor complicate matters with any of your future

## Chapter 2 | Get Rid Of The Ghosts

love interests.

When you feel really ready to re-enter the dating arena and eradicate any 'ghosts' from the past, the next problem is possibly being 'ghosted'.

This phenomena of 'ghosting' is when someone romantically bursts your bubble by suddenly vanishing without any form of communication.

When sex has occurred early on in the relationship then most likely at least one of you will have considered this was easy, so will continue until boredom sets in. There probably was never any form of friendship or romance, simply lust that will quickly fade as this shallow partnership lacks genuine love.

You become just another notch on the bedpost and soon will be discounted, because your partner will be eager to move on to find another 'victim'.

Unfortunately most digital dating apps are notorious for promiscuous and/or sex-starved people. These apps are ideal platforms for those who wish to find someone for a no strings attached hookup, but it is only for lust and not love.

Although it is liberating to sometimes enjoy commitment-free sex, the confusion and heartache for the one party seeking a solid relationship can be tricky.

As it is so simplistic to break any quick connections with someone you just met, then 'ghosting' becomes far too commonplace.

This happens for a plethora of reasons such as avoiding conflict, commitment issues, the fact there's no real spark between you, the fear of rejection, lack of respect or just that they haven't got time nor

## Chapter 2 | Get Rid Of The Ghosts

the inclination for the next steps that should be romance.

Cutting off contact is often the quickest and most effective way to part without the fallout of a break-up, which at least protects one party's well-being. Yet it can also have a detrimental effect on the other party, who has been 'ghosted' without explanation.

If you met your love interest on a dating app, be prepared to learn that you were probably just one of maybe dozens that were chatted up. Now you've been dismissed because someone else has probably been considered an 'upgrade'. Don't allow yourself to be in such a vulnerable position again, and it is best to avoid these apps at all costs.

Should you believe that there is a *bona fide* future for the two of you, it's best to give them some breathing space for a week or two. Then send a clear message, via text or email, that highlights how much you enjoyed your romantic episode but would now like to get to know them as a person.

Be patient by allowing this love interest to go off the grid for a short period, and if there's no response to your message then don't allow it to become a big deal. Pull yourself together and realize that it is their loss rather than yours. You can channel your love and devotion towards someone much better who is worth your attention. If it was far from genuine then they won't afford you the courtesy of a reply.

Stepping back is imperative here. If you are ignored then block them and cut all ties, otherwise they could become a 'ghost' from your past and jeopardize any future romance.

Understandably you may feel deflated and perplexed. Yet it is

## Chapter 2 | Get Rid Of The Ghosts

much better to know early on than six months down the line that this person disrespects you and selfishly only thinks about themself.

Life is a learning curve, and generally we all learn from our mistakes. You've only invested a short amount of time and learned the hard way from this bad experience.

If you can avoid 'ghosts' from the past, and can cope with being 'ghosted' then you're a step closer to finding a meaningful romantic relationship.

Start to visualize being in an exclusive partnership that is solid, and be ready to commit to regularly spending time together with a potential love interest.

You will obviously be seeking someone that you find devilishly attractive, and rightly so because part of being a sexual being is sharing passionate and pleasurable moments. However, you should try to find some common ground beyond the bedroom to potentially kick-start any new relationship. A personality match is just as important as a physical attraction, so don't already limit yourself to just those who possess outer beauty.

## Chapter 3 | Where To Start Hunting

Once you possess the motivation for seeking a loving relationship then be aware that romance can be complicated. It becomes incredibly spectacular when it runs smoothly.

You will no doubt in the past have thought what's the point of finding love, while you've been slowly waiting in the wings as far as a new romance is concerned.

Your dream date is unlikely to come knocking on your door and sweep you off your feet. Finding someone special isn't down to 'lady luck', so why gamble on sitting at home and daydreaming about the perfect person suddenly appearing?

You will continue to get absolutely nowhere until you have the inclination and desire to get out there to approach singletons. This is your opportunity in life to discover whether they could become your potential partner.

Be bold and engage in conversation without coming across too keen or desperate, because that will only put them off big time.

## Chapter 3 | Where To Start Hunting

For whatever reason you are re-evaluating your non-existent romantic life, which is often down to peer pressure or hitting a certain age, because you desire more out of life.

The first thing is to absolutely know what you want, rather than what you don't want. What aspects do you truly desire? You need to be clear about seeking a specific type of potential partner to fulfill your romantic needs and be prepared to compromise.

Once you have narrowed that down then you could contemplate borrowing a dog — from a friend or family member. As a man's best friend is meant to be a dog (not quite up to diamonds being a girl's best friend), then striking up a conversation with the aid of a furry friend can be an easy experience.

While in touch with friends and close family members, be direct and ask them who they imagine you being with romantically next. You could be pleasantly surprised when they offer to play Cupid by asking if they can arrange a blind date for you. If they don't offer then please ask them to keep their eyes peeled, and be patient. That's a massive step up from dating apps, and of course so much safer.

You may already have plenty of attention from potential partners, although more often than not singletons fall down the trap of staying stuck in the 'friend zone' instead of becoming romantically involved. If this is the case you'll definitely need to alter your tactics, and ask yourself why this keeps happening.

If you are set in a pattern of regularly hanging out with someone that you have romantic feelings for, but are making zero progress

## Chapter 3 | Where To Start Hunting

towards a possible loving relationship, then no doubt you are stuck in the 'friend zone'.

Familiarity breeds contempt, and will lead to the slow death of a glimmer of romance between you. It's essential to steer your relationship from being far too casual and making it feel like just friends.

Put in the effort to plan in advance any potential meetings, and look at changing it from the usual places you go. Forget hooking up for coffee, a drink or a bite to eat. Make this love interest feel special by offering some more thrilling options about where and when to meet.

Focus on adding some personalized conversation during your rendezvous, by subtly dropping their interests and any hot topics into conversation, to show yourself as attentive.

Make it blatantly clear from your attire that it's not just a casual catch-up as friends. Being well-groomed won't go unnoticed, and this potential partner will no doubt start dressing up to meet you in future.

Follow up your 'friend zone' dates by not disappearing off the radar after each meeting, regardless of how it went. If you want to see more of this possible partner then try offering more new experiences for your next rendezvous. It needs to be a meeting that offers some value to this love interest, to keep things moving and fresh.

Finding a common interest can hook in a potential romantic partner, but don't forget to also subtly project your interest through body language as well.

Should you still find yourself in a flirt-free zone during your 'friend zone' dates, you will definitely need to inject some flirty fun to spice

# Chapter 3 | Where To Start Hunting

things up. Knowing when to subtly touch and/or brush against the body will show that you like your date. You've got the green light to start moving forward if any of these actions are reciprocated, because generally speaking no one will physically touch someone unless they like them.

However, liking someone and being romantically interested are so very different. It's vital to understand this, and act accordingly with respect.

In time this person will realize that not only are you considerate, but that you are serious about spending time together. Once the penny drops you can comfortably reveal your feelings, and explain that you believe you could make a good couple.

Aside from potential love interests with friends, you need to realistically establish the sort of person you genuinely envisage yourself to be romantically involved with. It's no use trying to punch way above your level.

To attract this type of partner you need to be near them, as well as consider a change or update to your appearance for new inner confidence. A polished version of you is an amazing investment of time, money and effort. This upgraded version will add a new spring in your step that people will notice.

Giving off the right vibes and brimming with confidence will dramatically help you. Especially as singletons are extremely astute and can easily pick up any whiff of desperation, so could instantly reject you if you are unhappy, lacking confidence or self-esteem.

# Chapter 3 | Where To Start Hunting

If you possess the feel-good factor, and can start loving yourself with some new things, you can easily become more noticeable and therefore seem attractive to others.

The quick-fix choice of finding singletons is by checking out bars, as alcohol gives people Dutch courage. Only frequent bars as long as you don't feel frightened and lost when there.

But like everything in life you need to be fully prepared, so undertake some research and implement a plan about which bars are suitable. Always take into consideration your age group and the age of the clientele attracted to the bars you fancy visiting.

You're definitely going to be out of practice with conversation openers, so polish up your chat-up lines and opening gambits before you venture off to any bars. Stand out from the crowd with something different but say nothing cheesy, keep eye contact, smile and see if you can start a conversation.

Showing respect and a sense of humor will help. Just avoid being so narrow-minded and shallow by only talking to the best-looking singletons. The outer beauty may be the initial attraction, but never forget that inner beauty will not fade in time like good looks sadly do.

However, you could be placing yourself in a tricky scenario of going out to these bars as you seek romance. Singletons are often out drinking because they are angry and upset about being rejected by their former partner.

The attraction of bars being full of singletons arguably means easy pickings, but are these the type of people you really wish to meet for

## Chapter 3 | Where To Start Hunting

romance or are you merely being reckless?

It's worth considering signing up for some classes or clubs where you can meet new people, and with a mutual interest the conversation should easily flow.

Joining a gym, where you can also get yourself physically fit, are usually filled with recently single people so worth a shot. They often have classes where you can fine-tune your mind and physique as well as meet like-minded singletons.

Showing confidence and introducing some romantic gestures should be your starting block wherever you meet new singletons. Don't forget that both genders enjoy the thrill of the chase, so be courageous when trying to pursue a relationship.

As mass media portrays aspirational sugar-coated romances, created solely for entertainment purposes, you can clearly learn from these. There are always tips to hunt down someone who could potentially turn out to be your lifelong partner.

If you want an easier life then such simple scenarios, like shopping and walking a dog, offer you the chance to meet suitable singletons.

Supermarkets are ideal places to meet single people. Lingering where they sell ready-made meals, the snack sections and alcohol aisles are where singletons will be regularly shopping. Make phone calls to friends while there if you need to play the waiting game for someone to catch your eye.

It all depends on the type of person you wish to capture your heart, and obviously where they hang out when you go hunting for romance.

# Chapter 3 | Where To Start Hunting

Stepping into the comfort of their environment is where you are best to start looking. But it's far easier hunting for love in pairs, whether you are the hunter or hunted as far as romance is concerned.

The process of putting yourself out there through friends and family, and/or by initiating conversation with strangers, means you are looking in different arenas to those that have previously failed for you.

Molding ourselves to form a solid partnership is never going to be easy. As we get older this becomes much more difficult. Now should be the time to act, rather than keep waiting for the perfect person to suddenly materialize.

# Chapter 4 | Spark A Conversation

Getting a date is a simple process, but landing a suitable date is much more difficult.

It's far better to first value yourself and decide whether you'll settle for just any old date, or whether you want much more from life. If it's the latter then your desire will be to land a top quality date.

The secret to sorting out a good quality date is to firstly find some sort of foundation to build a potential relationship. If you can meet a singleton that you find physically attractive, who possesses at least one mutual interest, then at least this potential love interest has started to tick your boxes.

Yet finding this sort of suitable person to date is not a simple task. You may be required to spark a conversation completely out of the blue. The very best way to start a conversation with a stranger is by creating a scenario, so that they can begin to get interested in you.

It's natural to feel nervous when you've got romantic feelings for someone. Yet there are numerous ways to approach what you consider

## Chapter 4 | Spark A Conversation

to be a good-looking person to initiate a conversation, although that's largely dependent on the environment and any possible mutual interests.

Initially you must introduce the basics. Namely by flashing a genuine smile, showing positive body language and adding subtle communication to collectively indicate that you find this person attractive.

However, it's crucial to also show them that they offer value. This means it is best to ask them for some advice. It's very simple. You can just enquire about the time, show the need for a lighter for your cigarette/cigar or even query where they got their scent from because you couldn't help but notice how great it smells. With these three approaches you have generated a basic interest to grab their immediate attention with ease.

Once in conversation just take your time to try to build up a rapport. Show your interest by playfully touching their arm if appropriate, ideally if they make you laugh or you wish to reiterate something positive that was said.

Should you possess enough confidence then you can always go down the route of introducing chat-up lines. The majority of singletons would be flattered to be chatted up, and if you go down the route of using cheesy chat-up lines at least laugh at them to show you possess a sense of humor.

Should you fear the chat-up line approach, there are other basic expressions to get moving such as "That watch looks fantastic on you, what's the brand as I'm intrigued?"

# Chapter 4 | Spark A Conversation

It's imperative to always state whatever you say "on you", otherwise you are referring to an inanimate object and nothing to really do with this person.

If you believe that you are too shy for these, the best bet is to grab eye contact by standing near this love interest — but only within their peripheral vision. Don't reveal your entire face, just let them see your profile. Slowly catch a glimpse of them every now and then, to offer a teaser of you. Any singleton with confidence will smile or even approach you, which makes life so much easier for you to begin chatting.

Lacking confidence is an unattractive trait, so you need to improve your confidence otherwise others could soon see that you lack self-esteem. This means that they could take advantage of you, or immediately lose interest in you as a potential date.

Self confidence is only a state of mind, which you must develop to improve your chances in the dating world. Whatever happened in the past, even if your confidence was knocked by a silly comment from an ex, you now need to start afresh with a clean sheet.

Negative energy is a waste of energy, a traditional Jamaican adage. This is an expression that you should begin to employ as you move forwards. Visualize what you're aiming for overall, and stick to maintaining a positive mindset.

You can't help but gain immense confidence when you have the feel-good factor about yourself, which will inspire you to keep looking after yourself.

By concentrating on looking after yourself — such as dressing

## Chapter 4 | Spark A Conversation

better, having a healthy diet, sticking to a good grooming regime, relaxing (listening to music, meditation or watching television etc) and undertaking regular exercise — you'll accept and recognise yourself as the person that you genuinely wish to be.

Good looks alone aren't enough to land a meaningful date, so don't rely on simply making yourself look attractive. You really don't want to be stuck with someone who's one dimensional.

Should you be a hopeless romantic then you'll only be seeking a love interest who possesses Hollywood looks, and keen on enjoying a candlelit dinner.

Yet the reality factor needs to come into play, so that you don't try to date those who aren't on the same level as you — either in terms of education, emotional baggage, finances, looks and so forth.

Men are visual creatures, so they do initially need someone who is pleasing on the eye. Generally speaking, men are not as shallow as they're often portrayed. Deep down they are like women, who want their special someone to possess good character.

Once you start to appreciate yourself then others will too, which makes it much simpler to find an emotional connection with a potential partner. Positive personality traits, including optimism and strong self-esteem, are going to make you more attractive overall.

Maybe the reason you have yet to meet 'the one' is because you're a hopeless romantic, are too fussy, have been overthinking love and relationships or are looking in the wrong places to meet a potential partner.

# Chapter 4 | Spark A Conversation

In the modern world we're all being judged by those around us. Taking care of your appearance will attract the right sort of people if you are in a suitable environment. The more interesting that you appear to the world, the greater the odds of singletons wishing to know you better.

As a man's best friend is perceived to be a dog, then if you want to organically grab some attention do consider borrowing a dog from a family member, friend or even a work colleague. In such a relaxed environment it should be easy enough to strike up a conversation with a stranger when furry friends take a liking to each other. You can feel more comfortable striking a conversation in this situation when a dog is involved.

Yet having a dog near you is only an opening gambit. You'll need to show your love interest that you're expressing a romantic interest by introducing positive body language rather than being forthright or manipulating the conversion.

This is your opportunity to get the ball rolling, by briefly taking the lead when meeting a new person that you believe you could really take a fancy to romantically.

The way forward is when you chat, try to mention some of your hobbies and interests to garner whether this potential love interest also likes any of these. If the bait is taken then you should swiftly suggest doing the same activity together. Having a similar passion about something is a brilliant basis to begin building a relationship.

It's best to visit places where you have a genuine passion and there

## Chapter 4 | Spark A Conversation

will be singletons — whether it's an art gallery, sports club, swimming pool etc. You won't feel so nervous in these places as you'll naturally feel happy in these environments. Therefore it becomes pretty easy to start a conversation. You'll be able to convey confidence as you have knowledge about these places.

Supermarkets tend to be choc-a-bloc of incredibly friendly and jolly people. It's a great place to use some seemingly innocent chat-up lines, and in time you'll be happy to initiate a conversation with a stranger that appears attractive.

You can easily make conversation inside a supermarket by performing a variety of tricks when a potential love interest appears, although check that this person is alone and single (take a quick look to see that there's no engagement or wedding ring). The best tricks include: hanging around the frozen meals and trying to engage in conversation by asking for advice about meals for one; ensuring that you accidentally bump into their trolley then apologize by touching this person on the arm or by handing them a compliment about their taste in food/drink in their basket or trolley, and; waiting in the alcohol aisle, so when you see this person again ask if they have tried a specific bottle of spirits or wine before boldly making the suggestion of drinking it together sometime at a bar or on a picnic.

Once you feel more confident you'll realize what you can offer a relationship. This is when it's best to ask some close friends if they know of any suitable singletons that they can introduce you to — you could be delighted by their results of playing Cupid.

# Chapter 4 | Spark A Conversation

Don't forget that what you're seeking deep down is a long-term potential partner rather than just a date.

A good indication at the start of a budding relationship is when you value each other, so give your undivided attention by genuinely listening.

Someone who listens will surprise you after a few dates — such as remembering your favorite drink, holiday destination, scent etc. This type of love interest is a keeper.

Even if there's not an instant spark you should give someone like this time to blossom, because you two could possibly develop a long-term loving partnership.

It's always worth subtly letting any singletons that you've been keen to get to know them. This can be achieved by flashing them a quick smile, but then withdrawing your blatant interest. They should realize that you're interested in them from this.

The subtle use of clever body language can also reap rich rewards. Go and stand near the person you like, but with your back to them while you speak to someone else. This is when you need a friend to be your accomplice. If this singleton you like seems interested in you then you'll notice a glance to try to catch your eye. Your friend will be the only face seen, and they can gauge for you whether or not you're wasting your time on this potential love interest.

If you are garnering some romantic vibes you should just very slowly turn around, so that you're gradually becoming more visible to this person. The objective is to get within their peripheral vision,

# Chapter 4 | Spark A Conversation

which makes it easier for you to open the channels of communication.

Practice how to start a conversation calmly and confidently. It's important to learn how to take out the fear factor so that it's not an intense experience, although this could take time.

Many singletons fail to find true love because they opt to never talk to someone they like due to a fear of rejection. Overcoming any form of nervousness is essential, which often can be overcome by just taking a deep breath and not overthinking.

Anyone who overanalyzes lacks confidence, which is an unattractive trait. Putting yourself out there may be taking a risk. This is a positive attribute, which proves that you've been courageous enough to try to initiate a conversation.

The odds aren't stacked in the favor of those who think they'll be rejected by trying to start a conversation with a potential love interest.

Believing that you're worthy of someone's attention will convey confidence, and can almost make you feel careless. The longer you prolong approaching someone you truly like then the more awkward it's going to feel, and because of this a proper conversation may never occur.

There's no need to make the whole approach harder on yourself, so avoid being focused on the possibility of failure and rejection.

Just be yourself, interact and listen. Pay attention and focus on the words your love interest utters, rather than them, will pay dividend**s.**

Making positive eye contact the right way, with the occasional glance and looking away just before they could lock eyes with you, is

# Chapter 4 | Spark A Conversation

also going to create interest.

By holding their gaze for only a second longer than you would normally as if it was accidental is a real game-changer. This kind of eye contact moves from a glance to downright flirting, and you will both know it.

Eye contact flirting is often undervalued and rarely referred to. Making eye contact when talking to your potential love interest oozes confidence. It also helps the conversation become deeper, which greatly enhances your chance at making a genuine connection.

Direct eye contact triggers the release of oxytocin, considered to be the love hormone, which can create a sense of intimacy. This opens the doors to starting a conversation, and you never know where that may lead.

Trying to find a romance organically means that you firstly have to start to love yourself and then become proud and sexy. This means that you'll be giving off the right vibes, which will soon have potential love interests eager to make the first move to speak to you instead of you doing all the hard work.

When sweet romance does develop, over time it should move to that amazing experience of being lovey-dovey. This is your ultimate goal, which once achieved will greatly enrich your romantic life.

## Chapter 5 | Fancy Flirting

When it comes to flirting, there has to be some incentive for you to make the other person possess a desire to participate in chatting.

Before you go for broke you should pay attention to the details of the surroundings, where the love interest is and how you can tempt them into some sort of conversation.

The fear factor of rejection tends to put most singletons off trying to start a flirty conversation. Any love interest targets may decide to look into their phone or wander off if you approach them to try and chat up — unless, of course, you are blessed with outstanding devilishly good looks.

As well as the words you utter to a stranger, the way that you deliver these is crucial to be successful. Consider the speed, tone and volume to be appropriate to the surroundings.

Any opening line, which invites a stranger to share something about themselves, tends to work wonders.

An injection of humor can also help, so maybe try one of these:

## Chapter 5 | Fancy Flirting

- "Do you find it sexy when someone makes the first move or should I wait for you to do it yourself?";

- "I can't figure out how I should begin this conversation. With a compliment about how amazing you look? Introduce a cheeky chat-up line or say a simple hi how are you? What would you prefer?" and;

- "Sorry to intrude, I couldn't help but notice you. I wondered if you fancied some company for a quick drink?"

The reality is that although strangers will take immense care of themselves to end up immaculately groomed, most would prefer for someone to actually be interested in who they are rather than just what they look like.

Men, as purely visual creatures, are naturally going to be drawn by good looks. It should not be overlooked that over time it is looks that fade but character won't.

A huge difference between the two genders, generally speaking, is that men tend to look at relationships for the short-term while women often prefer long-term partnerships.

Too many men believe that a highly sexual opening line will get them the girl of their dreams. However, the sort of lady who responds to these sort of cheap chat-up lines are not going to be the kind of woman that their mothers will approve of. That also means that there's little mileage for a long-term, meaningful relationship.

# Chapter 5 | Fancy Flirting

For both sexes, there's nothing wrong with flirty chat-up lines if used as friendly teasing and joking around.

Give any of these quirky ones a shot:

- "Are you religious? It's just that you seem to be the answer to all of my prayers.";

- "Do you believe in love at first sight? Or shall I walk past again?";

- "I would say God Bless you, but it appears that he already did.";

- "If I ask you on a date, will your answer be exactly the same as your answer to this question?" and;

- "It seems that there's something wrong with my phone… it doesn't have your number in it."

An old 'trick' that has worked since the 1980s, and gets incredibly positive results, involves bringing in a friend to help you out. After you've exchanged eye contact with a potential love interest, keep your distance and instead send your friend towards the stranger.

This friend needs to be close enough to be able to smell the scent of this love interest, must exchange glances and smiles with this stranger before signaling to you that it's time to make a move.

The moment has arrived for you to make initial contact. Casually

## Chapter 5 | Fancy Flirting

wander up towards the stranger and point at your friend before asking: "Is that man/woman bothering you?"

Even though the most likely response will be a surprised "No", you have been bold and gallant. You can then be cheeky enough to politely ask: "In that case would you mind if I bothered you?"

Unless you come across as creepy or repulsive, then in all probability you're going to be invited to join this love interest for a chat.

If you can be intriguing to this stranger it will be more important than looking like a gorgeous Hollywood actor. Some exceptional opening lines to start the conversation moving include:

"It seems like there will be beautiful blue skies all weekend. How are you planning to take advantage of the sunshine?;

"You look like an outdoors person, so where would you recommend for a beach/a hike/a swim?" and;

"What sort of trouble are you getting into this weekend?"

If you're going to be courageous enough to go for the kill and ask this love interest out on a proper date, you must have something to offer apart from your company to show your value.

It's vital to be fully prepared, by offering two options rather than the standard yes or no response to the same sort of question regularly heard of "fancy going for a drink?" Focus on letting this stranger know that you are thoughtful and generous. Ideally you could ask: "It would be lovely to get to know you more, fancy going for a drink and a dance on Saturday night or can I buy you Sunday Dinner?"

# Chapter 5 | Fancy Flirting

Typical friendly teasing and joking around with each other is a popular flirting technique that works wonders.

For those who are ready to flirt, but constantly getting stuck in the 'friend zone', it's definitely time to change your tactics.

Familiarity breeds contempt, and leads to the slow death of romance even between married couples. So between a potential couple it's even more difficult if neither of you have been brave enough to outrageously flirt.

Should you and your love interest be set in a pattern of regularly hanging out, but are making zero progression towards a relationship, then indeed you are seemingly trapped in a 'friend zone'.

Aim to never contact any love interest in a nonchalant matter, such as leaving it until late in the evening to suggest meeting up. This kind of approach, which is very common, is far too casual and will often make your 'friend' feel like an afterthought.

Instead plan any potential dates in advance. Make this 'friend' start to feel special by taking the effort and pushing for two options about where and when to meet. This plan will soon pay dividends as in time it will come across that you are considerate and serious about seeing this potential love interest.

By taking the time to research and suggest going to some events, of course you know the interests of this 'friend'. There's a strong possibility that this person will realize from your words and actions that you're interested romantically about spending time together. This at least will stop you worrying that it is always about being together

## Chapter 5 | Fancy Flirting

just as 'friends'.

You can make it blatantly clear from your attire on your date that it's not just a casual catch up as 'friends'. Making an effort is worthwhile as anyone who is well-groomed and smells terrific will be noticed, by your 'friend' and others.

Whether it is a date with a stranger or someone in a 'friend zone' with you, it's imperative to focus on adding some personalized conversion when you meet.

Nowadays it's simple to unearth people's interests and hobbies thanks to social media platforms. Researching their taste in music, travel, tv shows etc means that you can subtly drop these topics into conversation. Remember that for the first couple of dates the man should be undertaking 70 percent listening and 30 percent talking, which allows you to size each other up while flirting and trying to read each other's body language.

After a date it's vital to not disappear off the radar, regardless of how it went. Keep your reputation intact for being a decent person, even if your date went horribly wrong and giving subsequent silent treatment seems appropriate.

Should you find yourself in a flirt-free zone during any dates, inject some flirty fun to spice things up.

Knowing when to subtly touch and/or brush someone's body definitely indicates that you like your date. You'll both be smiling if your love interest reciprocates this physical touch, as generally speaking no one will touch a date unless they like them.

## Chapter 5 | Fancy Flirting

However, liking and being romantically interested are very different, so learn to understand this and act accordingly with respect.

Fine-tuning flirting skills should automatically be updated throughout your life, similar to modernizing your appearance and attire.

However, you aren't alone in re-evaluating your amorous advances. Many singletons find themselves way out of practice after they have lost their romantic mojo.

Even toying with making flirtatious conversations with virtual strangers is going to be unnerving. The dating scene is becoming a quagmire as chance encounters appear to be the thing of the past in this day and age.

As sexual beings we all seek that magic spark with someone special to complete our own love jigsaw, but a certain amount of flirting is necessary to connect with someone.

If you feel too shy to make contact with someone you like or previously dated, it's best to let them know you are attracted to them via text message. Trying to kick-off a potential romance via text messages can easily trigger things off.

Rather than playing text tennis for months you can send a message, when appropriate, that reads: "Want to have this conversation in person?"

The answer that your love interest sends will ultimately determine whether or not it's just flirty fun that will never materialize into a potential date.

If you manage to land a date, in the morning send something to your love interest to maintain the mystery and interest. For example,

## Chapter 5 | Fancy Flirting

"You'll love the outfit I will wear tonight".

Whatever happens, don't continue the conversation nor respond to any questions about this subject as you must remain enigmatic.

If you want to be flirty to a total stranger then it's best to be bold and break the touch barrier early on with a gentle touch on the arm. This reiterates that you are interested.

Next step is to throw in some genuine compliments, which should boost their confidence. Brighten their day by telling them how much their jewelry/outfit/shoes suit them and match their eyes/hair/smile.

Never forget that most singletons have pretty much been starved of attention for so long that a subtle form of physical touch and a compliment will be highly welcomed. If you are honest and direct with someone that you're romantically interested in then it can work wonders.

The best bet, face-to-face, you can state is: "I seem to have lost the art of flirting, do you think I can get it back?"

The response will determine whether there are sparks flying or not. You can be frank and suggest exchanging phone numbers (should you not already be texting this love interest) if there appears to be a mutual connection.

Before you get out there to flirt, focus on smartening yourself up for dates. Smell good, dress age appropriately and practice your smile in the mirror. Then you will know whether you're a turn on or a turn off.

Flirting is about building up the emotional connection, which

## Chapter 5 | Fancy Flirting

fuels both attraction and trust. Once you have built this connection it can work to your advantage, by enabling you to potentially spend time together on dates. It could be part of your journey to find the perfect partner forever.

# Chapter 6 | Securing Second Dates

Singletons seeking true love will be desperately aiming to go out on a second date, third date and many more as romance blossoms.

Grabbing a second date is not as simplistic as it seems in today's modern era. With so many digital dating options, finding love has literally turned into a conveyor belt of singletons that are swiftly judged on a plethora of criteria such as emotional baggage, looks and wealth.

What deeply motivates us as human beings is the fact that we must have something planned, so need an event or occasion to look forward to like birthdays, festive seasons, holidays and indeed dates.

Blind dates, recommended by someone close to you, can surprisingly work out as long as expectations aren't too high. These suit some people but not others, but at least offers a sense of purpose to look forward to.

First dates must be perceived as the polite 'getting to know you' stage rather than be considered a 'hot date'. Otherwise excessively high

## Chapter 6 | Securing Second Dates

expectations may just crumble when it comes to the actual rendezvous.

When an initial date has been planned, it's naturally an exciting time with plenty to look forward to. Although you may be truly buzzing, it's best not to go around telling everyone about this upcoming date.

There are two main reasons for this, namely if there's no mutual spark between you and just in case the date fails to materialize. You don't want to have to spend time telling people that it has gone pear-shaped and be giving out negative vibes.

If you are wanting to give out positive vibes, which will happen when you have secured a second date and want the world to know how happy you are, there's some groundwork to be undertaken before your first date.

As you'll wish to subtly impress on your initial date, the best way to prepare is to attempt to find out more about your date. These should include the minimum of their hobbies, interests, where they like to hang out or visit.

Finding a mutual interest is the glue that holds a couple together in the early days of courting. With so many social media channels easily accessible, it should be pretty easy to do your homework to unearth relevant information.

It's best not to delve too deeply about your love interest, otherwise you may let slip about something you saw on their social media profile. The chances are your date will also have checked out your social media platforms, so delete or hide anything that could potentially be off-putting to your date.

# Chapter 6 | Securing Second Dates

By undertaking some research on topics that your date is passionate about, you're armed with enough information to come across as knowledgeable. This alone should be enough to keep the conversation flowing about a mutual interest.

It's imperative to prepare yourself both mentally and physically for this date. Although it's an exhilarating experience, it can be an ordeal overall for the very first get-together.

Mentally, you can use visual tricks before the date to reiterate to yourself that it will go smoothly. This is a method that many top-class athletes employ to be extremely successful.

Start, when you have some spare time, to envisage where you will go, what genuine compliments you might give, what you will wear and so forth. When it comes to the first date you won't feel nervous if you can maintain the momentum of these visualizations, and you certainly won't come across like an overexcited puppy dog either.

Physically you have a perfect opportunity to make the best of yourself before your first date. Work your way from top to bottom with an improved grooming regime, ensuring that you moisturize your skin both during the day and the evening.

As part of any grooming overhaul, there's no need to splash the cash but do invest in some good scent. You don't want to come across as smelling too overpowering during your date, just use a subtle scent that you genuinely like.

If you're unsure which scent to wear then it's time to ask those in your age bracket what type of sensual scent they prefer, and also

## Chapter 6 | Securing Second Dates

quiz those who work in a perfume/aftershave shop for their trusted opinion. Bear in mind that the smell of citrus is known to increase blood flow to the sexual organs, so test out a grapefruit or lemon scent before deciding on your purchase.

As you certainly don't want to turn up for your date smelling the same, or even similar, to others at the venue there's a trick that can distinguish you. Use one of your favorite scents as a base coat, and top it up with your new (and probably more sophisticated) choice.

Once you've discovered the best scent for you, it's time to start making this your signature smell. Just don't forget to wear it lighter during the day. This will energize you. After a while you're likely to become a head-turner, as you'll constantly smell great with this combination of two scents.

Preparing for a date means that you need to concentrate from the waist upwards. This area is going to be noticed the most, as it's highly probable that you'll be sitting down. Ensure that your hair looks really great and is super clean.

If you truly wish to make a big impression then you should get your haircut somewhere that you know offers top class styles before the date. This could result in exactly the same style that you already sport, or a visit there may improve your appearance.

Physically, you need to look and feel confident on a date. Many singletons tend to try losing a bit of weight before their first date. There's no right nor wrong method, it has to be about what makes you happy. Whether that means buying new accessories, clothes or shoes depends on you. However, don't try to portray yourself as anyone but yourself. If you're happy as you are then there's no reason to suddenly start running miles to get fitter.

Another vital aspect to prepare is to ensure that you practice your smile in the mirror. Best to try to learn to smile with your eyes, which is not easy but will pay dividends.

When you break into a smile on your first date, just let it appear slowly as this will come across as genuine. Your date will soon warm to you as your smile has built-in instant trust.

To further build up trust, and show your intentions, you can dish out a compliment when appropriate but only if you genuinely mean it. The best example to state is: "You're looking especially attractive tonight". This instantly offers the feel-good factor, and should put your date at ease.

Navigating your way through the nerve-wracking first date means you have to avoid the pitfalls, which includes making a *faux pas* by mentioning an ex.

There are literally hundreds of suitable questions to pose on a first date. This isn't a job interview, you don't need to know about their former lovers, pets, which vehicle they drive and so forth. Those boring aspects will only kill the romantic vibe, and if you two begin to date then all will be revealed over time.

Should the subject of former romances be raised, use a distraction question by asking: "What roles do love and affection play in your life at the moment?"

# Chapter 6 | Securing Second Dates

It's imperative for a man not to reveal too much about himself on this initial date, instead remain a little bit mysterious rather than evasive. The secret on any first date is for the man to be a great listener by only talking around 30 percent of the time, leaving the lion's share of talking to the lady.

By making the lady realize the next day that she didn't ask certain questions means that she's likely to be keen for a second date, even if it's just to learn more. This is because women tend to be more inquisitive than men.

The objective on a first date is to make a resounding impression on the person that you've devoted time, effort and energy to.

Some thoughtful questions will help detract from talking about the nuances of everyday life of being you, which should help to reveal your date's personality and hopefully make you an interesting subject.

If you're going out for dinner try asking: "Given the choice of any living person, who would you most desire to be your dinner guest?" This is a real conversation starter.

Everyone loves music, so you should be a real winner by posing a trio of quickfire questions: "When did you last sing to yourself? To someone else? What's your karaoke song?" These should immediately open up a lengthy chat. If you are perplexed by your date's age, their musical taste can be a great giveaway about their era of music.

To peel off the layers about their ambitions and future plans, which you really need to have in alignment to progress together, try asking: "Is there something that you've dreamed of doing for a long

## Chapter 6 | Securing Second Dates

time but haven't yet done?"

With any question posed, your date may fire back at you to answer the very same ones. Be fully prepared for that by being ready to come up with some first-class responses.

Confidence is the most important aspect that you need to take to your date, even if there's an initial spark or mutual interest. If you're confident about yourself, then you're most likely to attract the attention you desire and hopefully can land a second date.

For those who are trying to go low-key, or even trying to move from the 'friend zone', there's the option to have a movie night at one of your homes.

Popcorn is a terrific start to set the mood for a romantic rendezvous as you can share this and deliberately brush the hand of your date. There's also the added factors of popcorn smelling wonderful, potentially cooking it together to build up your rapport and the fact that it soaks up any alcohol should either of you feel nervous and overindulge with the booze.

You're only looking, as this is a first date, to enhance your date's desire towards you. Yet it's imperative to make the evening so pleasurable that your love interest should be biting at the bit to see you again.

There's a plethora of well-known aphrodisiac foods that can be used for seductive purposes, although some lesser-known snacks and smells are best to naturally arouse sexual instincts at this early stage.

Try to use as many aphrodisiac scents as you can get your hands on to hit the mark and help heighten senses for both of you.

## Chapter 6 | Securing Second Dates

Fresh popcorn, even if microwaved, along with the scent of warm donuts together provides uplifting and familiar smells that will cause an arousing effect.

Have some black liquorice and peppermints on hand, as both of these work wonders in terms of forbidden desire.

The sweet scent of liquorice, which derives from anise, enhances arousal. Ensure that your mints actually contain real peppermint oil, and that you suck on some of these about an hour before your date arrives. There was a reason why peppermint was named after the Greek nymph Minthe, the mistress of Pluto, who was the undisputed God of the underworld.

Vitality plays a huge part in human attraction, with the smell of citrus known to increase alertness and increase blood flow to the sexual organs.

Oranges and pink grapefruit are both used in top-end perfumes for a reason. Just before your date arrives gently rub these on your neck, wrists and down your arms to offer them a light citrus smell. Also leave some of these fruits in a bowl close to the sofa and/or coffee table in case you sit down together after a date or if you're watching a movie at home.

With this handful of inexpensive props you're set up for a delicious evening with a second helping extremely likely to be on your dating menu.

This initial date, wherever you spend it, is all about the expectation followed by sheer excitement. If there's a connection, a common interest

## Chapter 6 | Securing Second Dates

and/or a physical spark then you're most likely to be arranging a second date pretty sharpish.

There's tons of tell-tale signs on the first date that you need to pay attention to, such as body language and being asked "How long have you been single?" Both of these can determine whether your date is seriously interested in you.

By throwing in quips about doing things together will go a long way, and helps gauge whether there's a genuine interest. It's a sure sign that there's a potential future relationship when one person begins talking about doing things together in the future.

Don't reveal so much about yourself on your first date, otherwise there's very little point setting up a second date as your love interest will only hear the same things about you.

Hold back your funny stories and impressive details, instead offer a drip-drip feed of information to maintain your date's interest in you.

Although being a good listener on a first date is imperative, especially for men, there are other vital elements required. Laughing, nodding and smiling at what nuggets of information are revealed sends out positive vibes.

Yet you need to be totally genuine. Glean these details and store them in your brain so that you can prove you're being attentive by later referring to them in conversation on your first date.

Maybe you can use the information as a signal to sort out a second date. For example, if you start talking about how much you enjoy dancing and your date says: "I am pretty good. We should go

## Chapter 6 | Securing Second Dates

sometime and see who's the best dancer".

Be prepared to seize opportunities like this during your first date, building on that excitement of getting to know each other.

If you didn't get an opportunity to throw in suggestions for meeting up again, but would like another rendezvous, go for the kill by trying to close your date with the view to setting up a second date.

Either be courageous enough to ask them while you are still out together but give two options, rather than expecting a yes or no answer. The more modern yet vague approach is to let them know that you would like to go out again but not actually arranging anything.

Regardless of whether you push for a second date or act *blasé*, at the end of your first date let your love interest know that you had a great time — if you really did — and beam a beautiful smile (including a smile with your eyes) to reiterate it.

If you prefer to walk away it's best to message or call your date within an hour of going your separate ways with a caring message.

As dating is all about momentum, the key to securing a second date is about not waiting too long. It's no use playing games and being coy by waiting days before sending a message. Be direct and tell your date that you had fun so would like to see them again. However, you must offer an incentive to get them to agree to a second date.

Don't wait too long between your first and second date. As time passes without seeing each other, there's the risk that any chemistry you built will begin to fade.

Remember to ask: "What made you go on a second date with

## Chapter 6 | Securing Second Dates

me?" during your rendezvous. This will allow you to both suddenly feel relaxed as well as gauge whether a third date, and maybe more, is on the cards.

# Chapter 7 | Rose-Tinted Glasses

Love and romance isn't always like the movies, where everyone lives happily ever after. Yet these do help to paint a picture of relationships through the proverbial rose-tinted glasses.

This type of fairytale ending can exist for you, as long as you possess the ability to embrace a relationship. Ultimately, as individuals, we hold the key to our romantic destiny.

The overwhelming joy of romance is to feel special and valued, reciprocating these emotions to your partner. The better you perceive your partner, the more that you'll see them as a caring, exciting, gorgeous, interesting, special and talented person.

This paves the way for a formidable relationship, even if your partner isn't unique, because they are the most special person in the world to you. This loving relationship will only turn into a wondrous long-term romance if your partner feels the same way towards you.

After you've found what you perceive to be a genuine connection, there will be your 'partner enhancement' — seeing them through

## Chapter 7 | Rose-Tinted Glasses

rose-tinted glasses. This is natural to see past your love interest's flaws during the early stages of a relationship.

You identify myriad positives so initially will perceive them to be wildly attractive, charming, competent, considerate and talented.

As the romance progresses, this 'partner enhancement' wears off and gradually the majority of people cannot love their partner warts and all. This is when the relationship is on the slide, until it crashes and burns.

It's not that the relationship has gone sour when the flaws are more apparent, because you will still care for your partner and overall still see them in a positive light. It's just that there may be some verbal fights creeping in, and you may be irritated by their habits and quirks.

Once your rose-tinted glasses are off then it's essential to ensure that there's mutual respect, commitment and trust between the two of you if you both truly wish to move forward forever.

If you can develop a naturally strong bond over time, without being constantly annoyed by your love interest, it means that you're making the right sort of progress towards your fairytale ending.

Building a solid relationship over time is down to circumstances and life choices that you've made together. This helps to give you the belief that destiny threw you together.

If you're not in a relationship, you've probably been busy retreating into your comfort zone. Finding yourself set in your ways and following a rigid routine, coupled with keeping yourself in isolation too much

# Chapter 7 | Rose-Tinted Glasses

means that you have little chance of meeting a potential love interest. It's time to get out of any self-sufficient bubble to start meeting new faces with friends, maybe take a risk and join a club where you can mix with new friends.

When you're the new face at the club then you must make an impact. It's imperative to exude confidence and self-esteem in order to make yourself more attractive to any suitable singletons.

Unfortunately as we get older many unattached people believe that they're too old for dating. It should never be forgotten that love is for everyone, so try to embrace this amazing fact.

As we get wiser, learning from our relationship mistakes, we naturally have an increasingly self-protective defense mechanism. Anyone who has suffered repeated rejections will be wary.

Your main focus is finding someone suitable who can bring value to you, and that you can reciprocate this. Ideally your potential love interest should be your equal in terms of background, emotionally available, interests and looks.

Selecting a potential partner is not a simple task. As we get older and wiser it's natural to put our defenses up, but instead singletons often portray this by referring to themselves as "picky".

Being choosy is usually down to at least one previous unsatisfying relationship that broke down for whatever reason. We are bound to have had strong feelings for someone who hurt us emotionally, so there will be deep-rooted intimacy issues as well as the fear factor hurdle to overcome before a full-blown relationship evolves.

## Chapter 7 | Rose-Tinted Glasses

Chasing the ultimate dream love interest isn't a grown-up option, but as an experienced adult we may not necessarily want the love that we think we desire.

There's no need to desperately look out for this seemingly evasive perfect person because love often appears when we least expect it.

In the meantime we should continue to search for that special someone. The love interest is the one who values us for who we really are, that one person who can really make us happy and offers the ability to constantly bring a smile to our face.

The majority of single people are overzealous when it comes to trying to find the love of their life. Once they enter a romantic relationship, they sadly only have a very idealized version of love and romance.

If that's the case, these types of relationships can quickly crash and burn. This tends to be because one of the partners wants the romance to move along quicker than their love interest. Otherwise the rose-tinted glasses have suddenly vanished, with reality setting in as previously unseen flaws become far too much of an aggravation.

As individuals we all crave to find that remarkable someone who loves and respects us, so we often chase a relationship where there are zero doubts.

Generally speaking, ladies tend to be naturally attracted to men who ooze confidence and passion on top of leading seemingly exciting lives. Men who lack confidence, which can be easily tracked by a lack of eye-to-eye contact and/or poor posture, are a big turn off.

# Chapter 7 | Rose-Tinted Glasses

A stereotypical man, who possesses the physical traits of offering a high level of testosterone, catches the eye of certain admirers. Men who smile more gravitate towards being cooperative.

Yet globally speaking, those men who stand out to the majority of women boast a reasonably muscular frame, big nose, a good height, a square jaw and small eyes.

However, men who tend to be particularly attractive to women are blessed with more feminine features like full lips, a good head of hair, thin eyebrows and wide eyes.

To begin our quest for finding someone special, we need to learn about picking up vibes from non-verbal cues to avoid seeing them through rose-tinted glasses.

Attraction is based on appearance, character, smell and the way that our potential love interest presents themself.

Non-verbal cues can be broken down to just the basics of eye contact, facial expressions, fidgeting, grooming habits, personal space, posture, touching and tone of voice.

**Eyes |** Monitor eye contact. Refusing to look someone straight in the eye points towards lack of interest, although equally can mean lack of confidence. If your date's eyes are turned by someone other than you then this kind of creepiness of looking too much at someone else can be a massive turn off. Watch where your love interest's eyes wander when you meet up with some of your friends.

# Chapter 7 | Rose-Tinted Glasses

**Facial expressions |** Negative faces — such as being cross, sad or scowling — are always a turn off. The straightforward litmus test is to look at how your date reacts when unexpectedly meeting a couple of your friends in a bar or cafe. Take a glance to ascertain whether your love interest is angry, downbeat or even trying to be seductive.

**Fidgeting |** If the constant adjustment of jewelry or watch occurs, this means that your date feels insecure. Should one of their wrists be gripped and raised in front of their body, then this is a sure tell-tale sign that your love interest is feeling hurt or sad.

**Grooming |** A poor grooming regime screams a huge turn off to the majority of people. Dirty fingernails, sporting disheveled attire, greasy hair, being sweaty and smelling badly are all clues that your date urgently needs some TLC. You don't want to be their carer or parent. Take a closer look at how your love interest appears and, if necessary when you're in a strong relationship, offer to take your date for some grooming cosmetics and/or new clothes/footwear.

**Personal space |** Watch to see if your date intrudes on the personal space bubble of your friends, which could make them anxious. As you desire closeness from your love interest, any intrusion towards others is the total reverse for you and obviously oozes excitement for them rather than you. Check out if your date enjoys playing space invasion with your friends to make them feel uncomfortable, and if that's the case it seems that your love interest isn't a keeper.

# Chapter 7 | Rose-Tinted Glasses

**Posture |** Poor posture would point to the fact that any date really won't invest much effort in any future romantic encounters, or it could just be that they lack confidence. Watch out for any awkward stance, nervous shifting and/or slumped shoulders.

**Touch |** Regulating when to touch another person is very important. If there's any unwanted touching towards your friends by your date, then unless it's a tapped shoulder it's understandably likely to prove extremely irritating for you. Equally you may not have initially noticed how they handle themself. Keep an eye on whether your love interest constantly rubs or wrings their hands, keeps their hands in a pocket too long or crosses their arms. These actions could alienate you in the near future.

**Vocal tone |** Your date could easily become repellent over time with their tone of voice and other vocal cues. Check to see if you could get annoyed by their clearing of the throat, an unusual laugh, speaking too loudly or quietly, snorting etc.

Armed with these tips to read non-verbal body language means that you can avoid initially seeing your love interest through rose-tinted glasses. Take these cues into account and ensure that you act accordingly to your future needs.

If you firmly believe that you can live with their flaws, or can possibly modify your date's turn off traits then progress with the relationship to subtly improve them.

## Chapter 7 | Rose-Tinted Glasses

Work out whether continuing the relationship will prove beneficial to you on both a short-term and long-term basis, rather than letting this drift and continuing to wear rose-tinted glasses.

# Chapter 8 | Key To Happiness

People are happier when they're in love. They have an enviable aura about them because they took that leap of faith to find true love.

For most people the quick-fix solution to making life better, not necessarily happier, is to enter romantic relationships until they find one true love that's healthy for both parties.

Reciprocating romantic love can be a key to long-term happiness, but requires effort and patience. Seeking that special someone to bring excitement and joy into each other's lives is the ultimate dream for those who want love.

Good communication, shared interests and goals are terrific ingredients to achieve a fulfilling romantic partnership that's based on commitment, respect, trust and of course love.

Most people are aware of what goes into the mix yet they still struggle to find that seemingly elusive ideal person who will complement their life.

Bearing that in mind, dating apps offer an alternative of fun and

## Chapter 8 | Key To Happiness

frolics compared to initially meeting potential partners face-to-face to generate a spark. Generally speaking, digital dating is the easy option for those who seek sexual gratification rather than a loving relationship.

If you're one of those people who's more fired up about seeking lust and passion, then you need to consider what sort of love you truly desire in the long-term. Dating apps tend not to play host to the most reliable individuals. These tend to be a conveyor belt of singletons, which due to the format can allow them not to be particularly loyal nor truthful.

Regardless of whether you seek a slow-burning romantic relationship or a quick bit of fun and frolics, laying the foundations of self-love to find your goal is imperative.

We need to tune into vibrational alignment, through our emotions, with our energy and feelings. We need to self-love enough to recognise that we deserve much more out of our complex lives if we are truly seeking happiness and romance.

Self-love creates freedom within ourselves, allowing good things to happen organically. Without self-love we simply have needs and wants.

We make choices every day about energetic frequencies and aura. We can radiate anger, guilt, hatred and sadness at a low frequency to the polar opposite of compassion, joy, love and peace at a high frequency.

Opting for love we can magically attract good people and situations with little effort, which makes life feel right and happy.

In the dating world many singletons face a constant uphill battle to find someone with even a semblance of becoming their significant

# Chapter 8 | Key To Happiness

other, because of their constant and determined resistance.

That's why for those seeking romantic happiness, it's best to ask some close friends or family members if they know of any suitable singletons that they can introduce you to. The abundance of positive energy will create an added excitement from all parties involved.

Those who are initially too busy, too shy or distance is an issue, can always try video dating with someone who was recommended to them. This works equally well with someone met organically face-to-face.

It's simple enough to initially video chat with a potential love interest before meeting up in person for a proper date. Yet with smartphones and so many apps around, even video dating is viable in the early stages of a budding romantic relationship.

Video dates can be fun, as long as they are treated appropriately. The man has to take control of these video dates and show both his intentions and worth from the start.

Both of you need to ascertain your genuine value to a potential relationship. Take into account such factors as your age, assets, earning power, emotional baggage, intelligence, interests, looks etc.

By appreciating and understanding what each of you can offer a relationship it can be smooth sailing if you are compatible, happy with the relevant information and can show mutual commitment.

Over this video date you can subtly explore each other's value to a possible partnership, although over time will be armed with all of the information rather than just on the first date.

The best way forward is to agree on a set time to have dinner

## Chapter 8 | Key To Happiness

together via a video date, and dress to impress. Both parties should make their table dimly lit, maybe candles, so that the setting is romantic and not daunting.

Any true gentleman needs to be considerate and thoughtful to keep his date happy. He should either order a meal or bottle of wine for his date, so that they eat or drink the same thing during the video date. Otherwise, he could send some money via an app for his date to buy food, a bottle of wine or flowers.

Some ladies will want to reciprocate this gesture and wish to prove their worth, maybe by showcasing their culinary skills by making a meal to impress or sending their date some homemade biscuits or cakes.

Having something to look forward to together, albeit a long distant romantic meal, can excite the senses and be almost as good as a date in person. The video date is all about trying to sell yourself as a happy person with positive vibes, and someone who has the ability to make their date feel special.

Should any future dates also be forced to take place at a distance, you can always watch a movie together at the same time via your smartphones or emulate a bar setting while you enjoy a drink, snack and a video chat.

Once these video dates are over and all has gone well, then arranging to date in person will have built up immense excitement and sexual tension. With both parties having conducted romantic dates over video this will be quite unique, and started the ball rolling in the bid to find romance. Friends will no doubt be fascinated by how your

## Chapter 8 | Key To Happiness

relationship began and blossomed.

There are numerous ways that love illuminates happiness, but getting the basics right is imperative. Love needs to gradually build up. Firstly affectionately, then romantically before the intimate act of love making.

Loving someone sexually is not always as easy as people think. Many relationships, and indeed marriages, have ground to a sudden halt because they aren't sexually compatible despite appearing like the perfect couple.

There are numerous variations for couples not being sexually compatible that bring unhappiness in love. Obstacles include insecurity, lack of body confidence, medical issues (including medication), past sexual abuse, periods, personal or religious belief about sex and even the pain factor from love making.

The key to long-term sexual happiness in a loving relationship between the sheets is to mutually respect each other. We all need to have fun, relax and be appreciated before we can both be sexually fulfilled. Once we can work out what makes our partner feel happy, sexy and special then we can actually make that happen by being caring and attentive at every opportunity of love making.

Whether starting a new relationship or seeking a romance, to find happiness it's vital to focus on what we have rather than what we don't to create a positive state. It is a wake-up call for those who currently concentrate on what they don't have, as this will result in the ability to attract.

## Chapter 8 | Key To Happiness

Self-worth and the growth of a romantic relationship begins and ends with us as unique individuals. Love, which sits below our conscious awareness, is an emotion. As an emotion, love offers rational control. That means we can each decide when to fall in and out of love.

There's plenty of elements to finding romantic happiness after finding someone to share our life with. Positive body language and genuine compliments help to bring a smile to that special someone.

Showing empathy whenever there's a challenge, being attentive, caring and kind goes a long way towards happiness. Keeping realistic expectations of how each partner should behave is important, as any couple will have individual boundaries and flaws.

As human beings we are all ultimately seeking true love, not a love affair, as our key to prosperous romantic happiness. Like fruit love can develop, it can ripen but also love can go off, fade and vanish unless we can have the same hopes and dreams as our partner.

Prioritizing quality time together is important, but if that's not happening then explore more common interests to nurture your bond.

High quality communication is the make-or-break factor for a relationship to work. To meet a partner's relationship needs we must appreciate how they express and receive love. Active listening, shared feelings and needs are much more than just talking and having a laugh. To be happy means that both parties must feel heard and understood.

Creating a long-term loving relationship is about knowing your partner's feelings and needs, mutual commitment and respect to achieve the sort of happiness you both deserve.

# Chapter 9 | Ladder of Love

Ancient Greek philosopher Plato's *scala amoris,* more conventionally known as the 'ladder of love', is very specific on how to tackle finding romantic love in six stages.

His bold claim was that physical attraction is the initial first step on the rung of this 'ladder of love', which perfectly suits men as they are visual creatures.

This definition of love is purely about being triggered towards physical features and a particular type of body.

His *scala amoris* appears within Plato's philosophical book *Symposium*, translated from Greek to mean an after dinner booze session. It's devoted to love with Plato praising Eros, the Greek god of love and sexual desire.

His text, written in 385 BC, depicted a friendly contest of impromptu speeches from a group of distinguished men during a banquet to determine both the nature and purpose of love. Poet Agathon's esteemed guest list included playwright Aristophanes, physician Eryximachus,

## Chapter 9 | Ladder of Love

geographer Pausanius, academic prodigy Phaedrus and philosopher Socrates.

It was Socrates' speech, who summarized the words of all five guests, that was the climax of their enlightening evening. He supported the teachings of the priestess Diotima of Mantinea, whose view of love focused on the attraction to a particularly beautiful body.

This 'ladder of love', an obvious metaphor for the climb a lover was advised to make after finding someone physically attractive, was the guide for individuals towards genuine and fulfilling love.

A particular beautiful body is love's starting point. This refers to when we have first become aroused by the sight of someone, who we believe possesses individual beauty.

The assumption was that once lovers realize that most beautiful bodies are pretty similar, they can soon start to love physical beauty as opposed to just loving one person. Acknowledging that there are different kinds of body beauty, and recognizing those differences, meant there's a love for all bodies having moved beyond the passion for one particular beautiful body.

This evolution of love mapped out the third step on Plato's 'ladder of love'. Namely falling in love with beautiful hearts, minds and souls rather than physical features. By concentrating on character and moral qualities, love could be discovered through the recognition of spiritual beauty.

After loving the virtues of a beautiful soul, the next step was to contemplate the kind of practices, institutions and laws that are most

# Chapter 9 | Ladder of Love

productive of virtue to foster moral beauty.

This love for things was created by those with beautiful souls, who acknowledged how those creations fed their souls in return and benefited society through the arts and sciences. This admiration for more general things meant the original physical attraction that initiated love seemed unimportant and insignificant.

The penultimate step was the love for the creations that move society forward, sparking a desire to acquire new knowledge. Loving that knowledge was everywhere to be found, with the drive to acquire it for self-improvement and philosophical understanding.

The final piece in the jigsaw was the love for beauty itself, with the form of beauty deemed to be perfection. The theory was that it inspired perfect virtue in those who contemplated it.

This was the recognition of the beauty within ourselves, and acknowledging that it's the same beauty which connects us to all was this ultimate form of beauty. The ever present beauty of beauty in life that we can so easily love becomes love itself.

Physical attraction may have been the first step on the ladder to a love, and the appreciation of all that is beautiful in the universe, but the actual contemplation of the form of beauty is the final goal.

Plato believed that love could inspire people to appreciate all that is beautiful and divine in order to try to produce beauty.

Diotima told Socrates that if he ever reached the highest rung on the ladder, and contemplated the final stage of the form of beauty, he would never again be seduced by the physical attraction of beautiful

# Chapter 9 | Ladder of Love

youth.

Plato provided a one-sided model of love, which drew inspiration from the partner rather than ourselves. The sexual desire for a beautiful body turned into the desire for philosophical understanding to ultimately find genuine love.

Arthur Schopenhauer, a 19th-century German philosopher, firmly believed romantic love to be the greatest force in human life.

His opinion was that romantic love, which he considered to be an illusion, could drive people to death or even to the asylum.

Schopenhauer's school of thought was that love boiled down to the instinct of sex, installed in each individual. He claimed that love consumed us, with endless torment and danger, to disrupt regulated lives.

He was of the belief that ardent admiration and romantic electricity was simply down to the desire to repopulate.

Schopenhauer outrageously claimed that those unlucky enough to experience love could be driven mad.

In contrast Simone De Beauvoir formed half of an existentialist power couple with Jean-Paul Sartre in the long-term open relationship of these two French philosophers.

De Beauvoir's groundbreaking exploration of inequality and otherness in the Vatican-banned book *The Second Sex* was released in 1949.

Her line of thinking about love was comparing authentic and inauthentic love to loving inauthentically as an existential threat.

## Chapter 9 | Ladder of Love

De Beauvoir claimed that loving in bad faith was when believing that love will complete us as individuals or by losing ourselves with our love interest. This would result in losing ourselves as independent beings.

During the era of her published book, men were encouraged more than women to have interests and goals outside of their romantic relationships. This meant that women were particularly vulnerable to the dangers of inauthentic love.

Authentic love was considered to involve partnerships when both parties pursued dreams and interests outside of their relationship, yet appreciated their respective independence. This meant that neither party would be subordinate nor rely on their meaning of life because of their love for that partner.

Her advice was to pursue equality and independence in the relationship, but work on shared goals to create meaning together while retaining freedom.

As a Love Doctor, my initial advice to finding romantic love has always been for individuals to know their value prior to embarking on a relationship.

Many singletons wish to try and impress an individual that they know is out of their league in terms of age, looks and/or financial clout. Yet they still have the desire to pursue that 'prize' for the sheer thrill of the chase.

The expression 'birds of a feather flock together' shouldn't be overlooked, otherwise we can easily waste energy by chasing the

# Chapter 9 | Ladder of Love

impossible.

It's imperative for anyone seeking a meaningful relationship to know their value as a potential partner. Be honest about what can be offered, both on a short-term and long-term basis, before attempting to pursue a potential romance.

Being realistic in assessing our value and what we can offer prevents wasting our time, money and effort in chasing someone that will never be interested.

For those who have genuine affection and fondness for a potential love interest, the final reward of being in love can become more special if the romantic interest is reciprocated.

Rushing into a relationship should always be avoided, because generally speaking love is long-term whereas lust tends to be short-term.

Those eagerly seeking their next fix of feeling good trying to find love, thanks to those neurotransmitters dopamine and serotonin, will soon realize that it's just lust in the early stages of a relationship. In that case the romance will only run a natural length of time before the partnership starts to fall apart.

It's best to be patient and not try to impress too soon. Allow the relationship to develop into a slow-burning romance by showing respect at all times, and gradually grow as a couple.

Learning to build up a natural strong bonding through simple actions, such as caring behavior, can help kick-off the romance in style. Etiquette and good behavior always pays dividends with eye gazing, listening, nodding and smiling going a long way to express

## Chapter 9 | Ladder of Love

interest and show respect.

Avoid undertaking the same activities, as familiarity breeds contempt as well as boredom, once the dating begins. Trying to find something new to do will help keep the relationship fresh and add some sparkle.

The combination of these tips are powerful, and if employed properly will keep any romance alive with the true flame of love set to burn brightly.

# Chapter 10 | Think With Your Head, Love With Your Heart

Unfortunately for many seeking romantic love, it's true that history repeats itself firstly as a tragedy and then as a farce.

For the majority of those seeking romance, their head and heart are in perfect balance. Those after love tend to use their head to analyze emotions and feelings, yet it's the heart that's faster than the mind.

The head relies on logic, while the heart is focused on the state of emotions. Relying on logical thoughts is how we tackle life. Often life choices about romantic love are ruled by emotions.

To think with the head is natural, because all thoughts derive from the brain. To love with the heart is equally as natural. Any romantic thoughts play with the mind, but are strongly influenced by the heart.

When a heart beats faster in a relationship, whether new or not, this is down to a set of emotions caused by the mental aspects of arousal and stress.

The heart ultimately leads everyone towards the path of love and

## Chapter 10 | Think With Your Head, Love With Your Heart

romance. This state of the heart helps determine happiness, and also when things aren't quite so perfect. This intuition from the heart offers relentless compassion, empathy and love that is imperative to embark on a relationship.

However, there are limitations when it comes to decision-making by loving with the heart. That's why using brain power is so important, as it helps to weigh up the opportunities for personal growth in a loving relationship.

There are some stumbling blocks to loving with the heart. Those who keep making the same mistakes with relationship choices aren't learning from past experiences.

When emotions are running riot it means that there are no clear answers by following the heart. It's essential to not listen to the heart when distraught or upset, instead wait for calmness otherwise a huge mistake could possibly be made by making an impromptu decision.

There are people who allow their heart to overwhelm their mind, which can be frustrating for those who fancy being their genuine love interest. Generally speaking this type of individual is easy to spot because they are sensitive, slow at decision-making and easily get stressed out.

Yet those with the ability to love with their heart and think with their head are slightly different individuals. They tend to be extroverts and possess deep empathy.

Thinking with the head is a powerful tool, as decisions are based on logic and reason. When it comes to using the brain for relationship decision-making there can be so many variables that these confuse

# Chapter 10 | Think With Your Head, Love With Your Heart

and overwhelm the mind.

The heart allows individuals to think outside the box, rather than just be logical by concentrating on only using the mind for decision-making about romance. The heart can help individuals make the right decisions in relationships, and of course to ultimately find romantic love.

The decision-making process for love should be about all of the information gleaned from dates, which is why finding mutual interests and ambitions are important foundations for building up a meaningful relationship.

The heart can be the voice of reason that considers compassion, emotions, feelings, impulsiveness, kindness, love, moods, pain, pleasure and romance. It's more than just intuition, which is often applied to making decisions about relationships.

The brain is more mechanical about relationships. It is focused solely on logic and rationality about whether there is compatibility, in both the short-term and long-term.

So many relationships are like ships that pass in the night, and will run their course seemingly without rhyme nor reason. However, this is most likely down to not combining both thinking with the head and loving with the heart.

By only using the brain and not allowing the heart to guide, decision-making about relationships is just based on facts and without feelings or personal opinions. This means that there's little prospect of longevity for a romantic future.

Separating emotion from reasoning means that the head has ruled

# Chapter 10 | Think With Your Head, Love With Your Heart

the heart, which is perfect if logic reigning supreme is of paramount importance. It won't help create a passionate and romantic relationship just by weighing up the situation to embark on a partnership.

The mind can play tricks with the heart, and vice versa, so it is best to combine the two or suffer the consequences.

Numerous people fail to both follow their heart and think with their head, so they end up single. Plenty of these individuals sit waiting for the perfect partner while they pine after a former lover who left their relationship.

Time to heal from any hurt suffered needs to be considered, but there's little point in continuing to yearn for someone who broke our heart. Instead, it's time to reveal our true character by showing the world how to bounce back from such adversaries and then concentrate on self-improvement.

Anyone hurt by a failed previous relationship is understandably going to have some trepidation about finding romantic love again. Too many individuals avoid embarking on another romance for fear of another rejection.

It's essential to have a firm belief that falling in love can happen, we must just remain wary of living happily ever after.

For those who aren't able to easily move on from a broken relationship, there needs to be a line drawn under the past in order to move on with a romantic life. There's always the chance of finding an upgraded version of a previous partner.

If stuck in a rut about the past it's best to reflect on whose fault it

## Chapter 10 | Think With Your Head, Love With Your Heart

ended, and consider exactly why repairing the relationship was out of the question. Knowing these answers means that the problem can be erased from the mind, with all of the negativity forgotten. Negative energy is only going to be a waste of energy.

We learn from our experiences and mistakes, which covers both loving with the heart and thinking with the head. Two vital elements required for a wonderful long-term relationship.

Should the issue for the partnership breakdown have only been minor, and that person remains in the heart and in every thought, there's the potential to reignite the sparks if both parties believe that they were soulmates.

To repair the situation can be achieved by arranging a serious face-to-face chat in a public place, which avoids the pointing of fingers and raised voices, to discuss the possibility of rekindling the relationship.

There's only a chance of things working out if both parties can love with the heart and think with the head as well as accept responsibility for the split.

By determining what the realistic expectations are on a short-term and long-term basis, no time will be wasted. Hopefully the relationship won't crash and burn a second time as there is mutual commitment, respect and trust.

If nothing can be agreed, or one of you is given the brush off, it's best to focus on the future. Any tainted memories must be eradicated, otherwise confidence and self-esteem will be dented.

Never waste time thinking about the past, instead give someone

## Chapter 10 | Think With Your Head, Love With Your Heart

who is more worthy than a former partner a chance to find happiness and romantic love together with you.

The path of true love is never easy, with romance like the game of snakes and ladders to bring highs and sudden lows. Hearts can be broken on a temporary basis, but no one should ever allow their spirit to be broken as we all deserve to be loved.

Men are generally the more emotionally vulnerable gender, but try to disguise their natural flaw. This is why males tend to view sexual connection as a necessity, in order to feel safe in a romantic relationship.

Men, who usually have mountains of testosterone, will constantly be driven towards sexual thoughts. As long as males treat their partner with respect then all should be well in the romance department.

Sexual urges for men stem from physical signs, whether fantasy or real, as the male species is largely a visual creature. Females' thirst for lust is completely different to men, with their yearning for sex triggered by emotional feelings rather than physicality. So women are much more likely to love with their heart than men, although both genders need to initially find their love interest both attractive and desirable.

# Chapter 11 | Avoid Love Triangles

A 'love triangle', often depicted in Hollywood movies, is a fairly common issue. Although it tends to be a real problem when one of the trio involved is married. However, a genuine 'love triangle' only exists when there is reciprocation.

Due to the conveyor belt of singletons available on digital dating apps/websites, it's very easy to fall into the trap of being part of a 'love triangle'.

Bluntly speaking, if being presented with a straightforward choice of two potential partners and regularly speaking to both means the bets are being hedged and there's no commitment about connection.

Of course we all have the desire to build up a rapport until making that awkward decision of which love interest to pursue when there's more than one person available.

Yet so much depends upon whether the preference is to follow the heart or head to solve this dichotomy, or whether it's viable to love with the heart and think with the head.

# Chapter 11 | Avoid Love Triangles

This is when taking an honest look at our relationship history paves the way for a successful and meaningful partnership. Referring to the past, to see which route was previously followed, and being honest about whether those were the best decisions to create happiness will determine our future choices for both happiness and romantic love.

If following the heart has ended in tears over the years, or vice versa with the head, then it's pretty obvious that a change of plan is required. Taking into consideration this previous information presents a golden opportunity to improve our love life.

It's essential to be honest with our feelings and actions. If the initial love interest had sufficiently captured our heart and genuine interest, why even contemplate any form of communication with a second love interest?

One rule that breaks this is with exes. As long as the ex has been informed that any love will only be affection, rather than romantic or sexual, means conversations are plausible. However, that communication has to end once 'the one' has been discovered unless they happen to be friends or could become friends.

A former lover will never become part of a 'love triangle' unless there is unrequited love, in which case the friendship must grind down to a halt.

Allowing a second love interest to enter our lives is down to a plethora of reasons, such as an ego boost or emotional insecurity issues. Regardless of the reason, if someone has caught our eye or turned our head to such an extent that becoming embroiled in conversation and

## Chapter 11 | Avoid Love Triangles

possibly more is acceptable, then the original potential love interest should be shelved.

The initial possible partner simply didn't cut the mustard, but more importantly they shouldn't have their emotions played with.

Understandably, what started out as exhilarating fun by toying with two love interests will gradually become extremely risky. No doubt this charade boosts confidence and ego, but overall it is most likely to never be more than fun and frolics rather than a meaningful relationship.

Being unable to make a decision about which love interest to entertain romantically will always spell disaster. When bamboozled by this scenario it should be viewed that the real reason for the dilemma is that neither are good enough.

Be aware that the burning fire of passion could rapidly fizzle out with either if not both. As there's so little conviction about both potential partners during the early stages, it's best to stop wasting everyone's time. Accepting someone who doesn't tick all the boxes, and never will, is most likely to end in tears.

Yet choosing to be with just one of these love interests is a bold choice. Should a short-term relationship fail to work out as expected, it's not guaranteed that the other person will be prepared to hang around to be your back-up after being rejected.

It's alway best to concentrate on only one love interest and save the drama. That is unless all three of you are extremely adventurous and fancy a *ménage à trois*.

## Chapter 11 | Avoid Love Triangles

Acting flirtatious is something that keeps a romance bubbling, without this then it will peter out and develop into just being friends. Looking at how someone's flirting has altered over time is a quick way to determine who is a better bet than the other person. This might not need to be analyzed as the majority of relationships just come to a natural closure.

Of course anyone who pushes the physical boundaries in the early stages needs to be gone completely, unless it's genuine love and not lust.

Once one person has been favored and picked to date properly there's a guilt-free future ahead. By being faithful, loyal and trustworthy — excellent traits for a loving partnership — means that the special someone was picked for a potential long-term relationship. Obviously it's best that this person never learns there was a rival.

When something was needed to spice up a partnership that went stale, unfortunately a relationship can break down because of one person cheating. This creates an unwanted 'love triangle'.

It's always devastating for any loving relationship to come crashing down, but much worse when there's a third person involved.

After the euphoria has died down, and one partner has appreciated their mistake of cheating, it's pretty commonplace for the person who ran into someone else's arms to suddenly have the urge to rekindle the relationship.

It can be tricky to forgive such a major error, but it shouldn't be overlooked that it could easily occur again. Before contemplating giving the partnership a second shot, the reality is to question what aspects

# Chapter 11 | Avoid Love Triangles

of the relationship would be better second time round.

The general knee-jerk reaction is acceptance when an ex reaches out to ask to press the reset button, despite having suffered immense heartache. This agony and pain can only really be overlooked if there's a huge void still to be filled after them, and there's a need to have this cheater back in our lives.

Anyone who wishes to beg for forgiveness and prove that they've changed, they need to offer to go on a vacation somewhere together.

A mini-cruise or beach break is a solid enticement to try to win back both the heart and trust, when apologies and explanations are rife following the huge regrets and bad behavior. After a natural time gap between lovers, it's imperative that any reunion is geared towards love rather than lust.

A break in public means that it's possible to fend off getting intimate as quickly as possible. Good communication and genuine empathy need to be displayed before falling into each other's arms and forgetting the past.

It's vital to size each other up and gauge the chemistry before having a heart-to-heart talk about both short-term and long-term aspirations. After the situation has been established it's imperative not to just go through the motions of lust. A vacation will allow enough time for any flaws and chinks in the armour of the person who cheated to rise to the surface.

By refusing to look in the rear view mirror and apportion blame, the best attitude is to remain positive and focus on the future. Only instinct

## Chapter 11 | Avoid Love Triangles

and logic can truly determine whether it's worth being committed to truly trust an ex to be in a long-term relationship once more.

Yet relationships tend not to work the second time round, due to the simple fact that there are sugar-coated high expectations for a second chance. The initial stages will be terribly exciting but, after three to six months, these thrills are very likely to have totally evaporated.

When a second bite at the cherry comes along, we have a three-month spell to get back on track in life and not dwell on the past. No other people can get involved with either party, otherwise it's a problematic 'love triangle'. Romantic relationships should be played out by two individuals, not three.

Life's too short to fall for people's romantic shenanigans. Eating foods that will make us naturally happy such as bananas, berries, coffee, dark chocolate, nuts, seeds and wasabi along with keeping our spirits high will result in being in a much better place and be ready for commitment without the intrusion of a 'love triangle'.

Any improved version of ourselves, mentally and physically, will attract the attention of other singletons over time.

Whatever our ultimate choice of love life is, there needs to be no power struggle and for no one to be stringing anyone along. Playing with people's emotions is cruel, and if anyone does that to someone that they proclaim to love then the simple choice is to run away from someone that will deliberately cause pain. This type of person is unworthy of devoting our attention, love and time to.

# Chapter 12 | Never Neglect

When we are in love there should be desire, excitement and intimacy in droves from both parties.

These aspects, alongside a longing until the couple are together, helps build the foundations for a romantic journey. Neglecting any of these essential ingredients in a loving relationship is foolhardy.

When a new partnership blossoms it can initially be a bed of roses. However, should the behavior from either party in a new relationship appear to be too comfortable in the early stages, these signs are pointing towards this failure of true love.

For those who suddenly experience this when dating then it's best to cut loose from the partnership. If one person is seemingly not too bothered about spending high-quality time with their love interest, the romance is already on the wane and won't evolve into a solid long-term relationship.

It's always best to seek someone who can provide the essential elements of personal growth as a couple. There must be encouragement

## Chapter 12 | Never Neglect

and support from both parties to make a loving relationship work. Often one party needs the motivation from their love interest to want to spend valuable time together.

A common occurrence of a new relationship breaking down is when one party starts to lose interest. This tends to happen following the 'honeymoon period', the time when the couple are initially together and cannot keep their hands off each other. The reality of being in an ailing relationship is usually when the man's hormones have settled down, with his excitement of finding true love swiftly vanishing.

There are ways to turn things around and rescue the relationship if this is happening. At least one party must reintroduce flirting and inject vigor. It's time to up the ante to try to recreate the great romance that was developing before this unexpected wane in interest.

The main focus for attempting to rekindle any potential partnership is for the couple to communicate and set goals, working in unison towards a long-term and meaningful relationship.

Yet it needs to be established whether this is just a waste of time and effort if one party seems disinterested. A frank and honest chat will provide the answer.

What will determine this is whether one party truly has the desire to be a long-term partner, or whether short-term pleasures of fun and frolics are of more interest. Stabilizing a romantic relationship through solid communication is imperative.

Genuine long-term love is not particularly easy to maintain for a plethora of reasons. A deep connection is required, as well as constant

# Chapter 12 | Never Neglect

respect towards each other and ever-evolving excellent communication skills.

Maintaining the same level of affection and commitment often falls apart within the first year. Many couples succumb to losing respect for each other by saying something way too personal, trying to deliberately hurt their love interest's emotions and feelings, when they really should have kept a lid on things.

Sadly the deep trust between a couple can swiftly be lost without a filter on words uttered in anger, which often ignites the start of the end of a potentially loving relationship.

Any partnership seems doomed when such hurtful words about character are rammed down the throat out of frustration. If this unacceptable behavior continues then understandably doubts surface, and it will appear that one of the parties is no longer in love because of the pain suffered from ill-chosen words.

It's not always easy to simply walk away. Unless things can be altered, and there's a genuine apology, it is best to split up as the immense pain will never ease and unfortunately the trust between the couple has been damaged forever.

Many couples, especially when at least one partner suffers from insecurity issues, allow an unhappy relationship to drift on in the vain hope that things will improve. This is unhealthy for both parties unless any problems are just a blip and there's going to be major changes initiated by the couple to find a resolution to save the romance. Neglecting the way to tackle potentially repairing a relationship will

# Chapter 12 | Never Neglect

ultimately end in disaster.

Only the two parties in a loving partnership can determine what is truly desired out of a romantic relationship. All of the time spent in a romance with the wrong person takes away the potential time that could be spent with the right person.

It's natural to feel sad when a relationship appears to have run its course. The previous sparks associated with being in love often evaporate as quickly as they appeared.

A partner may continue to deeply show love and affection, but lack the same caring and considerate characteristics shown during the early stages of dating. Being spontaneous may not suit one party, and over time couples need to accept that this can totally disappear because familiarity breeds contempt.

Yet one partner may be career-focused and working long hours in order to build a solid future in a projected long-term relationship. Any man who genuinely works long hours, and isn't giving out misinformation to play the field or to be out with friends, is more than likely to be a determined and loyal person. This is the type of man who desires long-term relationships, and the kind that women who want a forever partner should be seeking.

Obviously the intimacy aspect will require much more effort with a career-minded potential partner. Feeling neglected need not be an issue if one party can up the intensity to get things romantically moving in the right direction. A candlelit dinner, sporting a new scent and the occasional small gift for no particular reason (apart from genuine love)

# Chapter 12 | Never Neglect

are terrific gestures to show that you remain romantically interested.

Being neglected in a relationship is never pleasant, and can feel like a huge gap is missing despite any overwhelming demands of everyday life. To counteract any lack of time together as a couple, it's essential for one party to meticulously plan a wide range of dates and events to attend to make every moment count as loving partners.

All relationships take time to work and run smoothly. If both parties are prepared to make some extra effort when things aren't perfect, there's every chance that it can be smooth sailing in the near future.

Calculating whether there's enough love and devotion to keep things on track on top of avoiding neglect towards either party at all cost, can determine the future.

Ideally the reset button needs to be pressed to return to the early stages of the loving relationship that was so fulfilling. Yearning to be together and the sheer excitement of spending time as a couple will definitely help rekindle any romance.

Yet for singletons who find themselves at a crossroads without experiencing a meaningful relationship, it's important not to neglect what they can offer to a potential partner.

Before deciding the next stage on the journey of love, singletons must weigh up the past and focus on the future. What are the real barriers to easily finding a happy and loving romantic trip? What is preventing us from taking courageous steps to kickstart a romance? Personal circumstances must be taken into account before embarking on the next steps forward to find true love.

# Chapter 12 | Never Neglect

Offering value to a romantic relationship is vital. We all must consider what went wrong in the past and concentrate on how to create a new and improved version of ourselves. With some fine-tuning and tweaks the next meaningful relationship may truly become the last-ever partnership, because true love can be forever.

Self-improvement can be achieved financially, mentally, physically and spiritually. A better version of ourselves will alway generate attention, which is a confidence-booster and offers the feel-good factor. If we can't truly love ourselves, then how can we expect others to be bowled over?

Working on just appearances to meet the next love interest is unlikely to end in a perfect relationship, unless both parties are equally shallow. Looks fade over time, but character doesn't so working on self-improvement must be more than just good looks.

Long-term love requires quite a few essentials. To succeed the three Cs of caring, commitment and (good) communication is required from both partners.

Despite these three vital aspects, after meeting someone new it's essential not to neglect talking about long-term aspirations, desires, goals and mutual interests. Any relevant information gleaned can determine whether a long-term future together can be achieved.

For a potential partnership to blossom then a deep connection, rather than intimacy like the early stages, is required. If respect between a couple evaporates then solid communication skills necessary for a loving relationship are also likely to be sadly lacking.

Those who fancy a long-term relationship should, once they have

# Chapter 12 | Never Neglect

unearthed someone special, go to a public place once a month to discuss the partnership and plan some exciting things to undertake as a couple to keep the candle of romance burning. Expressing to each other how things have moved forward, and listening profusely to each other displays empathy and respect. Any seeds of doubt can easily be dismissed with this approach, which will help to keep the passion burning.

Couples who enjoy being together as much as possible will realize that they have a solid future ahead, and as a team they can overcome most obstacles. Those who neglect their partner to spend time with others are on a romantic downward spiral, which is going to come crashing down with a bang.

Singletons in a new relationship should never neglect future plans. It's best to be blunt and discuss hopes and dreams, as well as reiterate why both parties are so important to each other.

Couples obviously need to have the drive and passion to follow their path to success, but it's an ill-fitting relationship if support is missing from at least one party.

When there's an overwhelming desire to complement each other's future ambitions, this type of person is a keeper. They will never neglect the partnership, either on a short-term or long-term basis, as they can devote attention, love and time that a loving relationship warrants.

# Chapter 13 | Stick or Quit?

Finding genuine long-term love is never easy, and maintaining that level of affection and commitment often falls apart within the first year.

Unfortunately, when the 'honeymoon period' is well and truly over there's not much that can be done to repair the relationship.

When there's no longer the lusting over each other like a rash, because the hormones have settled down, the excitement of being in love really has worn off and hey presto the romantic bubble has burst.

For a potential partnership to blossom, a deep connection rather than intimacy is required. If respect from either party is fast evaporating, and the communication skills necessary for a relationship to flourish are sadly lacking, there's not much that can be done to salvage the romance.

Sometimes it can be something that one party did or said that suddenly caused more distance between a couple in a seemingly budding romantic relationship.

Partners sadly tend to lose respect for each other by saying something

# Chapter 13 | Stick or Quit?

personal, when they should have kept a lid on things. A personal attack about someone's physical traits is unacceptable, and often spells the start of the end. Whereas words about character need to be taken onboard, and changes should be made if necessary by both parties.

Once the deep trust is lost, this often ignites the end of a loving relationship. If neither party is truly making each other happy then a serious sit down and discussion about the relationship is urgently required.

By explaining that things appear to have moved backwards rather than forwards, asking a partner about how they feel is the starting block. This is also a wonderful get out of jail card to play, offering the chance to act accordingly once the love interest has expressed themself.

The expression of "If in doubt go without" should not be overlooked. This could be adhered to if there are any doubts about a romantic relationship lasting, and if either party is feeling miserable about the partnership.

Before any approach is made about discussing the situation, firstly consider what really has made the scenario so bad. It's time for self perception and reality. Are you the same person that your partner was so enamored with or has there been a big swing of change?

If neither party appears to be deeply in love, this signals an opportunity to make a break up comfortable. Cut the losses and agree to walk away from a relationship that is only causing at least one of you misery.

Failure to nip things in the bud and deal with this now could sadly

# Chapter 13 | Stick or Quit?

result in the romantic relationship drifting on and become unhealthy for both parties. It could even turn toxic. All of the time that someone is with the wrong person takes away the potential time that they could be spending with the right person.

It's imperative to determine whether this is just a blip for whatever reason — whether it is family, financial, health or work reasons. The ultimate question is would either party really miss each other if there was a split?

Often one party will feel that they are being neglected, but happy to settle for that. Keeping someone that can be trusted and relied on, despite the flames of romance having died down, is too often down to the simple fact that there would otherwise be a romantic gaping gap.

When couples who truly love each other are together as much as possible through choice, and appreciate that they have a solid future, they can overcome most obstacles. For those wondering whether there's a future in the early stages of a romantic relationship, things do not bode well for a lasting partnership.

If pining to see a love interest, and having the desire to spend time with them is occurring, then things appear good for the future. However, if that's not the case then any relationship really is on a downward spiral. It could come crashing down with a bang unless one party halts the relationship to ensure damage limitation.

On the other hand, if both partners are willing to try to alter in order to get things back on track, with some extra effort the relationship can definitely be rescued.

# Chapter 13 | Stick or Quit?

Prior to deciding on the potential next stage on any seemingly doomed journey of love, it's essential for couples to sit down and communicate their feelings in a public place. By being out among others means that any conflict should be curbed, but more importantly each party can listen to each other.

To build the foundations for a romantic journey together there must be desire, excitement and intimacy. Long-term love needs to include the three Cs — caring, commitment and (good) communication. By utilizing all of these offers the opportunity to rekindle and stabilize the relationship.

Yet if there's no longer the desire for a long-term future together, and one party isn't particularly upset should the romantic relationship end, this is a harsh conclusion.

One factor that comes to light in this scenario is whether either partner remains the same caring person that they were at the start of the romance. Both should be realistic, and then it's easy to accept this and either encourage personal growth as a couple or end an ailing romantic relationship.

Relationships will always be a rollercoaster ride, but trouble lies ahead if one person feels that they fell off the ride and failed to jump back on.

Any romance that has well and truly died a death is not worth trying to rekindle. Life is too short to be oblivious to the fact that if you're going through the motions of dating as friends, then most likely at least one party has been looking out for an upgrade for sometime.

# Chapter 13 | Stick or Quit?

If an effective split is required, gradually seeing less of each other will wind down the romance. Going two weeks without a date should either jolt one party to realize how much their love interest is missed, or it reiterates the fact that the romantic relationship has been doomed for some time.

Following an enforced two-week break signals the time for a talk in a neutral venue in public. This is when it can be explained that the partnership is no longer keeping you both happy, and that answers are required about long-term plans together without being a burden on each other. At least by tackling this in person allows each partner to read the body language, which may be a bombshell or a real relief.

For those not as courageous, it's best to end it all via a handwritten letter. Breaking up via email, social media platforms or text lacks class and respect.

When splitting up it's generally agreed — only with the sugar-coated version — to keep in touch, remain friends and go to events together. Realistically couples drift apart, and probably only make polite contact for each other's birthday and at Christmas time for a year or two.

Should neither party be particularly looking forward to spending time together, and the flirting has deserted them both, it's definitely time to draw a line under the relationship.

Obviously it's best to let down a partner gently. Following the basic rule of the two-one approach softens the blow. Give two positive pieces of information, lovely things about them as a person, before delivering

## Chapter 13 | Stick or Quit?

the knockout punch that it's over. Telling a love interest that there's no longer a feeling of being connected in the same way that loving couples appear to be connected is an easy option.

Add the fact that realistically the very thought of spending forever together is truly terrifying, then mention something that is of genuine interest that needs to be pursued — such as starting a new hobby, studying or traveling. That way the love interest is unlikely to try to get persuasive and ask for reconsideration as future plans are being organized.

Reiterate that although it might feel awkward, someone very different will ultimately make their life complete. Explain how much the time spent together will be treasured, and say thanks for the memories.

Otherwise, despite both realizing that the romance has hit the rocks and there's no longer much talking, there will simply be a relationship that relies on just having sex instead of the previous passionate love making. This shouldn't be an obligation, and seeing each other needs to come to an abrupt end sooner rather than later.

The best step forward with any romantic relationship that's lost its fizz is for one party to take the bull by the horns and tell their partner how they feel and what is wanted. This ends any time-wasting.

For those couples who continue to utter the words 'I love you' to each other for the sake of it, but don't truly mean it, means that they are just kidding themselves.

Acting flirtatious is something that keeps any romance bubbling. Without this the love will peter out and the relationship could develop

## Chapter 13 | Stick or Quit?

into just being friends.

Some partnerships just come to a natural closure, and run its course. Initially believing that there was something special is natural, but if there's no mileage then stop wasting any more time and affection as it will affect your self-esteem.

# Chapter 14 | Romance Is Not Dead

Romance has always been portrayed as being the most remarkable experience, as it's the process that makes the love between two people so spectacular.

Love and romance is certainly not always going to be so similar to the movies, where everyone lives happily ever after. The mass media definitely enjoys painting a picture of relationships through rose-tinted glasses.

Although these fairytale endings do exist, they can only occur if there's the deep desire to embrace a romantic relationship. Ultimately, as individuals, we are the ones who hold the key to our romantic destiny and should put the past behind us where it belongs.

So many people give up on romance because of their previous bad experience. It can take time to be ready to give love another chance. For many it's extremely difficult to trust again in a relationship, but for those who do find someone new for romance it's imperative to give them the clean slate that they warrant.

# Chapter 14 | Romance Is Not Dead

It's sensible to be more cautious with a future choice for a romantic partner if there's been previous heartache. Just because the last relationship didn't deliver a perfect ending isn't a good enough reason to avoid finding a new romantic partner.

We naturally have an increasingly self-protective defense mechanism, and over the years will have realized that repeated rejections have resulted in unhealthy attractions.

Yet it's not that complicated to focus on the future with renewed hope. The reality is that a long-lasting romance will only fully function between those in a loving relationship.

Finding the confidence to flirt with potential partners is the first step. Unless our emotions remain in tatters, in which case waiting for the heart to heal is vital.

When trying to find a meaningful relationship then initially we all need to be bitten by the bug of love and be swept off our feet. It's essential to not allow lust to be the overwhelming factor, as opposed to true love.

This is often easy to distinguish. For those who are unsure, it's best to consider what's the glue holding the couple together. If it's primarily mutual commitment, devotion and respect then this is love. If the relationship is solely based on passion, sadly this is unlikely to last as boredom with each other will eventually set in.

You cannot simply sit back and rely on the ideal partner appearing out of nowhere and then being romantic just because you're single.

Love and romance is all about commitment. For those who can't

# Chapter 14 | Romance Is Not Dead

commit to someone emotionally, the best bet is to step away from returning to the dating world and take a prolonged break. Too many singletons go through the motions of finding a romance just to appease peer pressure, which ultimately is likely to end in disaster and ruin self-esteem.

Only when we feel emotionally fearless is there any chance of a new, meaningful relationship blossoming. Focusing on finding someone who can bring value and is emotionally available is of paramount importance.

Going to the usual haunts for singletons of bars, clubs and restaurants may be buzzing. Yet these tend to be full of desperate-looking singletons who will be happy for any sort of attention, or alternatively they will be too picky so seem destined to remain forever single.

There are strategies that are not much of a gamble and can pay rich dividends for those who genuinely have the desire to meet that special someone organically.

It's easy to strike up a conversation with strangers when furry friends take a liking to each other. A man's best friend is considered to be a dog, so single men tend to enjoy bumping into other singletons who also have a dog. Borrow one from a family member, friend or even a work colleague if necessary. Any genuine caring nature for a four-legged friend will shine across, and with a beaming smile it's easy enough to spark an initial conversation. The two dogs may become friendly, which is the golden opportunity to suggest a play date for the pooches.

## Chapter 14 | Romance Is Not Dead

Everyday scenarios such as shopping and walking are great opportunities to meet suitable singletons. Don't be intimidated, we all admire confidence so feel free to approach people and make conversation. Supermarkets are brilliant places to meet the unattached, especially down the ready meals and snack sections, but check that there's no engagement/wedding rings or hovering partners before making an approach.

Any brief opportunity to initiate a conversation needs to be seized, but subtly let any potential partner be aware of your interest in them through body language and your availability to date.

Unfortunately the ongoing struggle to meet 'the one' is often down to overthinking love and relationships. To truly change things instantly, the first step is to narrow down the search to a specific type of partner to fulfill our romantic needs.

Love can occur at any time, and Cupid's arrow can hit our heart when we least expect it. This will be richly rewarding when it happens, and when we find that special someone the couple will really make each other happy and regularly bring a smile to each other.

Ideally we would love to meet a potential partner who's willing to pour out their heart and be unafraid to disclose how you make them feel once the romance has got going and the relationship has turned lovey-dovey. This is the super romantic scenario that appeals to virtually everyone, yet unearthing this kind of partner tends to be a scarcity and explains why there are so many singletons around.

Finding someone who wears their heart on their sleeve, and is

# Chapter 14 | Romance Is Not Dead

happy to give their undivided attention by genuinely listening, should be snapped up if they tick the other boxes.

Once in an established relationship, if romantic gestures have moved on from the basics of say bringing chocolates to gifts that are related to the information that has been relayed (such as a favorite drink, holiday destination, scent etc) then this is a keeper.

Romance isn't dead in this day and age. Both genders have an equal chance to take a romantic lead.

A guaranteed memorable evening could be a themed candlelit dinner with the music that matches the menu in the background (for example Cuban, Mexican, Italian or Spanish), with the host learning some romantic expressions in the foreign language.

Being a hopeless romantic often leaves hopes for a blossoming relationship dashed for men and ladies. Powerful yet sugar-coated romances are drummed into society through words and images, which are created solely for entertainment purposes. These are meant to be aspirational, so they aren't as run-of-the-mill in real life as they are on the big screen, books and magazines.

Yet there's the chance to take advantage of what's constantly portrayed in movies, so consider taking a leaf out of romantic comedies. It's pointless to keep expecting to bump into 'the one', or have them suddenly knock on your door. Be proactive, and hunt down that someone special that you're actually attracted to.

Naturally those who have been emotionally hurt in the past may have given up on romance, and even meeting new singletons. If that's

## Chapter 14 | Romance Is Not Dead

the case there's nothing wrong with only sticking to those singletons that you already know, although it narrows down the probability of a long-term romance.

Always avoid returning into the arms of an ex, which is the easy option, unless you were true soulmates and the reason for the split couldn't be avoided.

Even with singletons in your social circle — whether friends of friends, from a club/group, a work colleague etc — there are ways to give them the right signals for a potential romantic journey together.

For those who like to play mind games, there's an excellent way to impress a potential love interest that is already a familiar face. Organizing a general get-together of their friends or colleagues, but inviting this particular singleton last — at least 24 hours after everyone else — will confuse them.

By putting their nose out of joint this singleton may wish to make a concerted effort to grab your attention or simply impress you. However, you need to up the ante. At the event go up to the potential love interest and briefly explain that you always like to save the best for last before walking away with an air of mystery.

These words should prove to be captivating and perplexing in equal measures. No doubt this person will be eager to learn more and try to speak to you, so keep a distance but flash a friendly smile and prepare to be chased. The thrill of the chase for both of you could initiate the sparks that you desire, which could easily lead to a full-on relationship.

# Chapter 14 | Romance Is Not Dead

With a keen romantic interest in someone within your social circle, it's essential to try to find out more about their interests. This can be subtly found out from their friends, or even social media platforms.

Armed with these details, utilize this mutual interest to your advantage. This will be the bait to reel this singleton by researching the subject in order to engage in conversation. Even if it's something that you know inside out, be modest and reiterate that you aren't an expert about it so that this singleton can get enthusiastic with you about this common interest.

Once there's chemistry and the conversation is flowing with positive body language between the pair of you, then instead of pushing for a date make a romantic gesture.

Romantic gestures are ultimately unselfish gestures. The best way forward, to give an inkling that you like this person, is by buying a small gift. A terrific and thoughtful gift is a scented candle, which will last hours and help to make this person chill. When the aroma fills their room, they will be reminded of you.

Ensure that you possess exactly the same candle. This offers the opportunity to titillate this singleton by revealing that you have the same candle that you enjoy while relaxing in the bath. This information, if there's sexual chemistry building, makes it virtually impossible for this love interest to not think of you in the bath all chilled out. That scenario creates a perfect way to kick-start a potential amorous relationship.

Dreaming about meeting the perfect partner, who will ultimately

## Chapter 14 | Romance Is Not Dead

banish your days of being single, will remain a dream unless an effort is made to be proactive.

The word romantic was originally used in England to describe inventiveness in both literature and paintings. Feel free to be creative and unafraid to approach suitable singletons for the right reasons. Simply being a wallflower by waiting in the wings generally gets singletons nowhere, whereas oozing confidence and delivering romantic gestures offers the chance to land a lifelong partner.

# Chapter 15 | How To Hunt For Perfection

Whatever happens we must never dwell on the past, nor convince ourselves that we can't be madly in love and happy like we experienced in a previous romantic relationship.

Rest assured that millions of singletons who have suffered loneliness feel forced to re-evaluate their love life. This is due to both peer pressure and believing that a new partner will be an instant quick-fix solution.

Seemingly perfect romantic relationships come crashing down all over the globe. There are a plethora of reasons for this. Some include unforgivable infidelity, poor communication skills and boredom with each other — that can be just outgrowing each other or spending either too little or too much time together.

When we become isolated from the world of romance for too long, we should be aware that getting our head turned may take someone extremely special. This opens up the pitfall of seeking an upgrade simply based on looks alone. Naturally there needs to be some form

## Chapter 15 | How To Hunt For Perfection

of physical attraction, but it's also essential for a couple to also possess an emotional connection.

When hunting for the perfect partner it's best to forget the love at first sight scenario, which is so rare that it's best saved for the movies. Often it's lust that singletons are mistaking for love at first sight.

It's worth planning properly how to reach such a goal, as finding someone special is such a wonderful feeling when both partners are experiencing the early throes of being in love.

Things can always alter in the romantic department, and they will shift for singletons by starting to show belief that we are worthy material for a meaningful relationship. Yet it's the potential love interest's background, character and values that should be of paramount importance.

Perfect is a big word to put out there. The reality is that no-one can possibly be absolutely flawless, meaning that our first change has to stop having such high and possibly unrealistic standards.

There's no need to just settle for anyone nor drop high standards in order to start dating for the sake of it.

Being alone can be daunting for many singletons, who then feel pressured to seemingly settle for virtually anyone. The danger of being pushed into a half-hearted relationship is that there's a possibility that one of the parties could start to notice other singletons, which would mean that the partnership is on a slippery path by partly being forced from the very start.

Rather than rush into a romantic relationship we should embrace

## Chapter 15 | How To Hunt For Perfection

being alone overall. Socializing is the only way to break the habit of being alone, finding groups to join and potentially exploring new hobbies. This offers a chance to intrigue others and to start the path of loving ourselves.

Finding singletons with a common interest is the foundation for a solid future, whether initially as friends or there are the early elements of a romance.

Ensure that anyone singled out as a potential love interest doesn't sport a wedding ring (nor engagement ring). Also check that this isn't going to be a rebound relationship, because the last thing we ever want is to feel used, confused and wasting time with the wrong person.

Rather than have a scattergun approach, it's best to build up the rapport with only one potential partner at a time and explore whether we could actually envisage ourselves as a long-term couple.

Try to decide what makes this love interest as close to a perfect 10 in our eyes. Failure to consider this is costly, because no one really wishes to relentlessly repeat the process after a few weeks or months when this person doesn't meet our high expectations.

Before embarking on the early stages of flirting, it's worth utilizing any precious alone time by trying to create the perfect you. It's all very well seeking perfection from a love interest, but try to achieve being as close as possible to the flawless person that we wish to be.

Let any potential partner see we can show respect for ourselves and others, because in the early stages of a romance we all seek someone who we know will treat us well on a long-term basis.

# Chapter 15 | How To Hunt For Perfection

When it comes to traditional physical flirting — eye contact, handing out compliments, mirroring each other's movements, reading body language, smiling, touching etc — then it's imperative that these are up to scratch. Body language normally gives the game away about whether there's a mutual spark.

Yet we need to be armed with weapons in the dating world when searching for someone who could possibly be the perfect partner. We must utilize introducing small talk, show good intentions, polish up the humor and tick all the boxes as far as self-improvement is concerned.

Once someone special has come along there must be mutual respect. To get things moving along it's vital to prepare some bespoke compliments that are *bona fide,* and subtly deliver these over time. This information reveals that they've been on our mind, it will make them feel special and ensure that they'll realize their worth from these carefully chosen words.

Couples savor the feeling of wanting to learn about each other, which adds to the excitement of a new relationship. When it comes to revealing information about ourselves, it's best to solely reveal positive aspects in our life — family, friends, health, interests, wealth and so forth. This positive attitude gives off positive vibes, which should ultimately attract people towards us.

By altering our mindset to be the perfect partner will instill much-needed confidence. As long as confidence doesn't overflow into arrogance, it can be a real plus. Of course there also needs to be passion to maintain a meaningful relationship.

# Chapter 15 | How To Hunt For Perfection

Rome wasn't built in a day, so we should lay down the foundations for a future with love and romance by making ourselves fascinating rather than being overly fussy. Managing to overcome being picky, often because of a previous relationship, can result in being ready to commit to a long-term partnership.

To hunt down the perfect person forever it's vital to stop being so selective in the process for finding success, by thinking outside the superficial box of what the majority of singletons seek — which tends to be good looks. Never neglect the fact that looks fade over time but character will not.

It's imperative to be cautious about rushing into a relationship when only seeking true perfection, allowing good looks to play tricks with the mind.

Instead of relying on being shallow and just seeking specific physical requirements in a bid to find the ideal person, it's worth devoting time to research their interests for an ice breaker. Then narrow it down to those with our similar interests, which should help generate genuine high-quality conversation.

It's better to look 'under the bonnet', rather than staring adoringly at the outside beauty. Otherwise we may be served up the same sort of the cheesy compliments from an array of desperate singletons, who will forever remain unoriginal with their words — and repeat these to each and every single date to try to wow them.

Beauty is in the eye of the beholder, so only the whole package should be measured. Someone smoking hot with a less than favorable

## Chapter 15 | How To Hunt For Perfection

personality is not going to be deemed beautiful overall. Whereas an average-looking person with a sparkling character is going to be a much more attractive proposition in the long run.

We need more than a one-dimension relationship to be happy forever. Stop looking for potential love interests who turn heads like swivel chairs, just because of their good looks. Beauty is in the eye of the beholder, but everyone is beautiful in their own way.

The problem is that we live in a judgemental world, where we dismiss people within a few seconds based on their appearance. There isn't always the time to peel off the layers to discover character and personality. Yet true beauty has nothing to do with appearance, only the heart.

Connection is what a meaningful and loving long-term relationship will thrive on. Unearthing that special someone to settle down with is a huge commitment.

Everyone's ideal partner is more than likely a mirror version of us in terms of character and looks. It's best to avoid those who've always been driven by their career and previously too busy to commit to a relationship, as there's a strong probability that we will feel neglected over time by anyone who's previously been strapped for time.

Some relationships run like clockwork when the couple don't spend much time together. On the other hand some couples thrive by being in each other's pockets. Whatever the situation, it's all down to being in the right comfort zone and routine overall as it's horses for courses. It's also absolutely essential to never discuss work nor anything serious

# Chapter 15 | How To Hunt For Perfection

in the bedroom, as that area should be reserved for sleeping as well as fun and frolics.

As we get older we tend to appreciate life more and become wiser, resulting in naturally exuding confidence and high self-esteem — which will help make us appear more attractive when single.

When focused on trying to find a perfect partner, regardless of age, seek someone who can bring value to the relationship. Ideally this special someone should be an equal in terms of background, interests and looks as well as emotionally available.

Anyone who starts to desperately seek perfection for that seemingly elusive special someone is unlikely to find them. There's no need to drop high standards, just be realistic and never forget that love often appears when we least expect it.

For those who are quite particular and demanding, their type of partner mustn't frustrate them in the early stages of a relationship otherwise it will soon be curtains.

The majority of single people have a yearning to find the love of their life, and once they enter a romantic relationship tend to have a very idealized love. Yet this can come crashing down because one of the partners wants things to move along quicker than the other, or the rose-tinted glasses suddenly vanish as the 'honeymoon' period is over.

As individuals we all crave unearthing that special someone who loves and respects us.

Yet there will always be differences of opinion and ultimately problems in every partnership. These are usually caused by frustration,

## Chapter 15 | How To Hunt For Perfection

such as lack of intimacy, and/or situations that are causing hurt to one or both parties.

When there are issues and fights, if these arguments are making progress rather than one person being hellbent on trying to win then it's going in the right direction as a couple and the fights signify passion.

Don't make the mistake that for someone to be your perfect partner all you need is love. A lasting romantic relationship on the menu needs to have plenty of the right ingredients such as good communication, commitment, respect, sincerity, trust and understanding to help create the perfect dish of love.

When we are fortunate enough to find that someone special that we genuinely find amazing each and every day, then by constantly displaying dedication will help deliver that powerful and pure feeling of being in love.

The search for that perfect forever partner can be determined if we really do make each other deliriously happy, and are constantly able to bring a smile to each other's face, before commiting to a long-term relationship that could last a lifetime.

## Chapter 16 | Building Foundations For The Future

Properly preparing for a long-term and meaningful romantic relationship is essential for singletons to constantly look and feel confident in every aspect.

This paves the way for a potential partner to appreciate us. Obviously if we don't love ourselves then how can we expect a special someone to love us?

An underlying issue for couples is that they may no longer grab each other's attention like they did at the start of romance, which is often down to familiarity breeding contempt. Many singletons will recall this as the reason for the breakdown of at least one previous relationship.

To combat this we must always keep the partnership fresh, break from the norm by giving unexpected gifts and suggesting new experiences.

There's no need to splash the cash to show we care, it's much more

## Chapter 16 | Building Foundations For The Future

important to use carefully chosen words instead. Try uttering those special three words of "I love you" when appropriate, and explain from time to time the reasons for being in love with anyone who seems really to be that special someone.

When relationships aren't going as smoothly as we would like, it's worth suggesting future plans to establish the long-term future and where we stand in the mind of a partner.

This is simple enough to achieve in a subtle manner, and avoid the panic buttons like hinting that it would be wonderful to repeat something that was magical. Alternatively, we should go for the kill with a vital question such as "What do you look forward to experiencing with me?"

Determining what couples truly desire from a romantic relationship is rarely discussed. People, especially those with insecurity issues, tend to be content to allow their relationship to drift on. This is unhealthy.

Yet the fact of the matter is that all of the time we persist with the wrong person, takes away the invaluable time that we could be spending with the right person.

Personal growth as a couple must be relentlessly encouraged and supported by both parties in order for the romantic relationship to truly work and become forever.

Love and romance isn't all about looks, although as men are visual creatures there's bound to be shallow souls who may disagree.

Although many men can improve like fine wine, there's most likely to be the unwanted appearance of middle-age spread. This is

# Chapter 16 | Building Foundations For The Future

particularly common for ladies, and can dent both confidence and self-esteem. This is another reason why it's essential to showcase our unique character to any potential partners.

If romance was solely about looks, only those deemed to be universally stunning would ever be involved in loving relationships.

When the initial attraction, because of good looks, has faded then we appreciate the character of our chosen partner. This is because the relationship has developed from smoking good looks to the importance of the whole package.

We live in a world where most people demand instant results, which accounts for why we appear to be increasingly judging people within a matter of seconds.

To focus on the future of finding someone who could possibly be the perfect partner forever, we need to consider a makeover to reflect our true selves on the outside.

Celebrities and Hollywood stars periodically have to either reinvent themselves or undertake a makeover, which attracts new fans and gives them a confidence boost.

For those seeking a new romantic start, a makeover should comprise much more than a trendy haircut and a new set of accessories, clothes, footwear etc. It's our character and attitude that needs realigning.

When we meet any potential partner it's natural that they'll want to know about us. Yet by showing that we care about our appearance means that we'll discover more people being approachable.

Singletons whose self confidence has taken a beating over the years

# Chapter 16 | Building Foundations For The Future

should soon feel better in themselves by sporting different attire, hair and accessories. Positive comments from family, friends and work colleagues will help to introduce a spring in our step. These are the people who know us best, and they will notice any changes.

When spending money on upgrading ourselves it's important to concentrate on everything that will portray our appropriate age group and is in vogue. It should not be overlooked that taking pride in ourselves also means that grooming products require an upgrade for top-notch maintenance.

Finding completely different scents and investing in two signature smells that aren't overpowering, is a vital move. It shows that we care enough about ourselves. Picking out the correct scent needs feedback from people we trust, then it's time to sport separate daytime and evening/weekend smells.

We should only ever buy accessories, clothing, footwear and scent that makes us feel good and that we genuinely like. Far too many people spend big bucks on well-known brands just to impress others, but these soon become neglected when the novelty of showing off has died down. This can also be the scenario in a relationship, opting to date someone because of their looks alone.

As good looks and fabulous personalities don't always go hand-in-hand, we should stop only finding the best looking people attractive otherwise we could miss out on finding 'the one' by being shallow.

Before going out to try to meet the perfect potential partner, we

# Chapter 16 | Building Foundations For The Future

need to evaluate ourselves. Compiling a list of what are our 10 best things will instill confidence and self belief. When we value ourselves then others will follow suit. Being ourselves is definitely the best step forward, so that our character shines through.

Suitable singletons will soon be reacting differently, in a good way, and make us ready to dip our toes back into the pool of dating with aplomb if there's been a resurrection of our former happy self.

Now comes the hardest part, communicating with a possible love interest. It's time to scrap the unoriginal chat-up lines and instead be armed to unlock conversations with something newsworthy or fitting for the place where we mingle with singletons.

Being well-heeled is always going to be so much more attractive than someone who doesn't take interest in their appearance and personal hygiene. Ensure that you already have the advantage over other singletons, who are looking for love, and that you can justifiably feel great with a good grooming regime.

Don't appear too desperate or be overzealous. It's essential to not run before we can walk, instead take things step-by-step to allow any romance to transpire organically.

Romantic relationships are generally built around the 80/20 rule, which means that a man should chase the lady for 80 percent of the time until things are running smoothly. The 20 percent of chasing by females will only come into play if there remains a genuine interest.

Strong communication is a vital aspect in any growing romance,

## Chapter 16 | Building Foundations For The Future

yet written messages can easily get misconstrued and overanalyzed — so should be avoided at all costs, unless they are short and sweet.

When we are ready to explore the long-term future, ideally after at least 18 months together, and start seriously thinking about making a life with someone, then we should evaluate the current scenario. Is this partner our best friend and soulmate? Or just someone who wanted a storybook love affair, which was built on passion? The reality can either lead to having unearthed the perfect partner, or be a bitter blow that was overlooked.

Should things become pretty perfect, before considering marriage or moving in together, it's best to go down the route of asking advice from those who know us best.

Pose the important question of whether they envisage a long-term partnership between you two. Don't overlook the fact that men tend to prefer short-term relationships and long-term careers, whereas it's usually the reverse for women, which means you'll probably get totally different responses to your query.

Such a direct question to friends and family should result in upfront answers, which will help determine the future. However, some people will be jealous so won't reveal a true answer — be prepared for these.

If a happy future beckons this signals a new chapter, this offers the opportunity to continue — or even improve — our behavior to reflect genuine affection and devotion. Constantly being thoughtful, and letting a partner know how extremely special they are to us, are just some of the ways to make a romantic relationship work.

# Chapter 16 | Building Foundations For The Future

The very best gift we can ever give anyone that we love romantically is our time, so by making that our priority it paves the way for a potentially long and happy future together.

# Chapter 17 | Unearthing Our Soulmate

The ultimate love connection is without doubt a soulmate relationship. To discover such a deep and natural connection is an extremely rare find that should be grasped with both hands.

It's so powerful and richly rewarding that people will relentlessly react more positively towards us, as individuals and as a loving couple.

A true soulmate, which is someone who's going to have an everlasting impact on our life whether they are with us romantically or not, is tricky to find in the first place.

Unearthing a true soulmate can unquestionably be an emotional rollercoaster ride. Although a soulmate is ultimately our true love, we should always be prepared for a bumpy ride, because even soulmate relationships experience the general ups and downs in life.

It's imperative to believe that our soulmate exists out there. As we are all aware, Cupid can strike at any time. Love is pretty complex. It isn't delivered to us on a plate just because we believe that we deserve it. We have to continue to work at being loving, then we'll receive

## Chapter 17 | Unearthing Our Soulmate

love back in return.

The important truth about romantic relationships is that we must create love to nurture a soulmate connection.

An initial step, in preparing to find our soulmate, is to concentrate on ourselves. We must start to love everything about ourselves, although be realistic about our strengths and weaknesses. If we cannot fall in love with ourselves, how can we honestly expect someone to love us and stay with us as our forever partner?

Our every action, thought and word is a creation of us. We are the creator of our future, so brimming with a new-found confidence will work wonders to appear attractive.

Genuine smiles, confident body language and wearing clothes with assurance all add up to being noticed for the right reasons by a possible future love interest.

While seeking a soulmate it's not necessary for potential partners to both be cut from the same cloth, it's much more important for couples to possess a strong feeling of affinity and connection to complement each other in every way.

When romantically involved with someone special, we can quickly move through the gears to exceed being so incredibly happy to becoming ecstatic about life and love.

Once our rose-tinted glasses are no longer showing our partner to be nearly perfect, there's the harsh reality that who we consider to be our soulmate is far from an angel to have fallen from the heavens. This is when some vital factors need to come into play, if there's any

# Chapter 17 | Unearthing Our Soulmate

chance for a meaningful romantic relationship to continue.

To move forward forever, especially after the 'honeymoon' period has ended, there must be a trio of essential ingredients to ensure there are suitable foundations for a couple to stick together like glue. A lasting romantic relationship requires mutual commitment, respect and trust on top of keeping love and romance fresh with thoughtful gestures.

Solid romantic relationships have partners who truly possess the deep and burning desire to be together as often as possible. Initially at least one person will have struck the sparks then fanned the flames inside our heart. These flames will continue to burn if both parties can be fully committed to the loving relationship.

Should the fire fizzle out by one partner, the sad scenario is that our heart becomes a blazing ruin. The relationship is doomed despite reflecting on treasured times together.

Instead of attempting to repair it, it's best to think about the past for a while and then concentrate on the future of finding happiness with someone worthy of our attention, devotion and love.

When we get the signal that it's time to hit the reset button once again, wait to be emotionally ready before joining that wonderful experience on our personal journey to find a suitable soulmate.

Not everyone can experience a special soulmate connection, especially as a naturally strong bond can take time to develop.

Other types of soulmates can enter our life, but it's all down to timing and not always romance. We often like to sugar-coat it by firmly believing that destiny threw us together.

# Chapter 17 | Unearthing Our Soulmate

**Companion soulmate |** Friends essential to our lifetime journey. They challenge us to be real, love us with our flaws and will never abandon us in anger.

**Karmic soulmate |** This relationship doesn't require intimacy. The intent is to make a difference together and fully complement each other as a partnership.

**Kindred soulmate |** Sharing the same things by agreeing and disagreeing with love and affection, without any form of jealousy.

**Soul contract soulmate |** A deep law of attraction holds these two together forever by a common commitment.

**Soul crossing soulmate |** Even a brief encounter with someone who crosses our path can offer a lasting impact on the direction we choose.

These are all very well and good, but looking for clues that a soulmate romantic relationship could be blossoming is more important when trying to find a perfect partner forever.

A deep and profound bond, with a strong physical sensation, is a good starting point. So too is feeling like we've known our love interest forever, even though it's only been a few months. There are a plethora of other signs that maybe we've unearthed a true soulmate.

If we become increasingly more confident about ourselves since meeting this partner, then this is because they are making a genuine effort to ensure we feel good about ourselves. If we believe that this

## Chapter 17 | Unearthing Our Soulmate

person is a soulmate, we will have started to appreciate our own self-worth because of their impact on our life.

Other factors include being instantly completely comfortable around each other, feeling understood without any pressure, offering two-way empathy and following that all-important powerful gut feeling. These are crucial for those seeking a loving and meaningful long-term romantic relationship.

Disposable relationships seem to be the norm, partly due to digital dating, but these constant rejections are damaging for our confidence and self-esteem.

Because of the ease of being able to meet someone romantically online rather than in person, many ingredients required to find chemistry — such as body language, smell etc — are absent.

When on the lookout to find a true soulmate, it's vital to hunt down someone who would happily encourage us to develop and grow overall as a person.

In reality most single people who find true love and romance will either be caught by surprise when it arrives. On the other hand, far too many singletons will be content to simply settle for virtually anyone as their next partner in a desperate bid to be cared for and loved.

When we meet someone face-to-face and the relationship blooms, the huge difference between being just a couple and soulmates is that neither of us will give up on each other at the first sign of trouble.

As fun and frolics was possibly the reason for getting together, as opposed to a connection, then soulmates unite in order to work

# Chapter 17 | Unearthing Our Soulmate

through their challenges as a dream team.

When we are with our soulmate, we will gradually discover that we have become more alert and conscious of our surroundings. The energy from loving couples who are soulmates activates our senses, which is known as the butterfly effect.

If the person that we assume is our soulmate is tuned into our energies, and we feel a deep connection with them even from a distance, this is excellent news as our love interest has their energy focused on us at all times.

Some couples conclude that their connection is even stronger when they are apart for whatever reason. This points to destiny, which explains why they were put in each other's paths as soulmates.

If there's a magical romantic connection between a couple then often the sheer presence of our love interest can excite us, our heart rate increases and sometimes we get goosebumps with a mere touch on the arm.

When we are connected romantically, our heart rate tends to beat louder and faster in a positive way — the same feeling that we experience when we fall in love. Yet this heart rate increase phenomenon doesn't apply to everyone in love.

On the path to finding our soulmate we need to work on making ourselves a better catch, by being a more confident and happy person. However, we should never neglect the importance of needing to initially rely on chemistry rather than good looks.

What we must concentrate on finding is that indefinable connection

## Chapter 17 | Unearthing Our Soulmate

with someone. We will know when this individual is that special to us, as the feel-good factor remains when spending time together.

Possessing aspirations and expectations to bring to a future relationship, and into our life in general, can prove to be an asset to a potential partner.

We also need to find our own soul, because only after we have found our own soul can we truly find a soulmate. Our one and only true soulmate is that person with whom we are meant to be with for the rest of our living days.

Once we have found the seemingly perfect partner we have to work on ensuring it is smooth sailing. At the stage when couples are extremely comfortable with each other, and the romantic relationship is making steady progress, it's time to ensure that good communication keeps everything running smoothly.

We can only enjoy a successful forever relationship by both compromising. For longevity in any partnership it's of paramount importance for couples to approach communication with mutual honesty, openness, patience and understanding to continue their journey as true soulmates.

What we truly desire and deserve forever is unearthing our soulmate. Being soulmates offers incredible passion and romantic gestures in addition to both meeting equally on emotional, intellectual and spiritual levels.

A soulmate is the most intense type of romantic relationship that we will ever experience, so it should be cherished. It completes our life's

# Chapter 17 | Unearthing Our Soulmate

jigsaw of love when we discover a soulmate is that essential final piece.

Absolutely anyone can discover their true soulmate at any time, there are no barriers. As human beings we aren't programmed to be alone forever. The overall purpose of a romantic relationship is the challenge to grow together and to help our partner reach their full potential, which is why a soulmate works wonders in this situation.

# Chapter 18 | How To Keep Romance Alive

For all romantic relationships, to successfully achieve true love is heavily reliant on a daily commitment to each other and keeping dignity in our hearts.

We can experience the 'honeymoon' period, which psychologists refer to as the idealization phase, but that excitement of being together evaporates easily for some couples.

Others drift on without having any passion for their partner, which means both parties are effectively wasting each other's time as there's never going to be a really happy ending.

These early stages of a relationship is when we can try to convince ourselves that this latest love interest possesses most of the perfect characteristics that they truly can be our perfect partner forever.

Naturally everything seems extremely exciting during the early throes of a romantic relationship. The endorphins produced mean that we tend to be prepared to leap through hoops to try and prove

## Chapter 18 | How To Keep Romance Alive

that we are going to be their last ever lover.

These early days of love can actually just be lust. The relentless fun may last just a matter of weeks, months or years depending on the circumstances such as external pressures, lifestyles and proximity to each other.

When reality sets in, with bad habits and flaws suddenly becoming transparent, it can result in the previous nights of passion being replaced by a solid night's sleep and distance between couples.

This isn't down to the individuals changing, despite the constant claims to the contrary from couples when arguing. If the 'honeymoon' period comes crashing down, this is when it becomes apparent exactly who this potential partner really is. Unfortunately the love can begin to fade, or worse still completely disappear.

Just because the idealization phase has come to a sudden end doesn't mean that a long-term relationship is doomed. If the couple believe in each other, and are soulmates, it's simply a question of reigniting the spark into the partnership by being spontaneous and committed to making it work.

The secret to any successful long-term relationship is to accept and respect. We need to accept that our partner may not be quite the person who we originally thought we fell in love with.

We've not outgrown our love interest, so need to get the spark back into the romance. Introducing some fun elements, making unselfish gestures, trying unexpected new things and returning to places where we created memorable moments together will add an injection of zest

# Chapter 18 | How To Keep Romance Alive

into our love life.

With our ultimate goal being to find someone on a long-term basis, being confident and laidback are our best ways to prevent ourselves from looking desperate.

When it boils down to reality, and the thrill of meeting someone is starting to evaporate, we should ensure that we have more going on in our life than only being focused on a romantic relationship. Those who possess a full life tend to never worry about how to stop looking desperate.

It doesn't matter how attractive looking we are, any potential partner could run a mile if we ever come across as clingy, lonely or pathetic through our actions.

Some prime examples of appearing desperate include always being available to date, making too much contact, becoming over dependent and possessing low standards. Worse than all of these is pushing for a serious relationship early on unless it really is true love.

Many people will relish the opportunity to test our boundaries at the start of a relationship. We shouldn't allow them to overstep the mark like asking for naughty selfies, being a cheapskate and/or constantly turning up late for dates.

When we meet someone that we feel deserves our attention, and could prove to be our significant other, patience is a virtue.

Allowing a relationship to develop into a slow-burning romance, by showing respect at all times, permits love to gradually grow equally as a couple. Slowly building up a relationship will always prove beneficial

## Chapter 18 | How To Keep Romance Alive

on a long-term basis.

We should definitely not rush things nor try to impress too soon, otherwise the romance could be primarily built on lust or high expectations. Once that fades we could face the prospect of wanting to swiftly escape a whirlwind partnership.

There's rarely the need to rush things, but romance shouldn't be ticking along at a snail's pace either. Any lasting relationship is built on affection first, followed by romance and then it organically moves to the sexual connection over time.

It's essential to ensure that any love interest appreciates our worth to them. This means they value us, and in time we become so important to their happiness that they can't wait to spend time with us.

This is the reality rather than demanding such instant attraction that we can expect to fall in love at first sight. It may never happen, yet for others it can occur up to half-a-dozen times during their lifetime.

Many people are too dismissive about romance, and won't date unless it's love at first sight for them. These people tend to stay single for at least a decade but, unless they alter their attitude, will remain alone and romantically undesired for the rest of their life.

So let's get back to basics and start to show our worth as an attractive singleton and a potential long-term partner. It takes time and effort working towards a long-lasting relationship that's full of passion and respect.

We need to be confident, comfortable at approaching a potential love interest to initiate conversation and be able to show that we are

# Chapter 18 | How To Keep Romance Alive

fun without being dizzy or silly.

Flashing a quick smile instantly shows interest. Should there be mutual attraction then we will get glances. The best step is to encourage whoever we are out with to make us laugh. This laughter becomes infectious, showcasing ourselves as a happy person. It can also make a love interest perplexed by what's making us laugh.

It's imperative to give off the right body language signals to indicate that we are approachable, and are keen for either party to make the first move. Keeping our head high as we sit or standing straight and tall, darted glances and trying to make eye contact are great ways to flirt.

Once we have garnered some interest from a potential romantic partner, it's best to follow the classic male-female psychology of letting them chase us without playing hard to get.

Those singletons who appear too desperate tend to ask someone out at the drop of a hat and/or constantly make contact first with any love interests.

We need first to grab someone's attention in order to hook their interest. Evolution attracts people to high-value partners, so let the chase begin by sending the right signals that we are a valuable asset.

Don't neglect the adage of "Fools rush in where angels fear to tread". Any excitement shouldn't spill over into looking like we are desperate to find a romantic partner, especially as we all tend to smell that kind of desperation with ease.

Appearing truly desperate is if we show that we have a great need to be in a romantic relationship regardless of any obstacles. We may

# Chapter 18 | How To Keep Romance Alive

even give off the wrong vibes or come across as terribly insecure.

There are ways to utilize some simple body language tricks when meeting someone that interests us romantically. Pointing our body and toes towards a possible love interest offers subconscious cues that we're interested in this person as more than friends. Flashing our sweetest smile and tilting our head slightly forward is positive. Crossing our arms, leaning away or with legs crossed and pointing away are the sort of actions that give off negative vibes and indicate we have little interest in the person.

It takes two to tango. Start making much more of an effort if there's not been much romantic interest recently.

We should always utilize time away from a romance to upgrade ourselves, which allows us to be able to project the best-looking version of ourselves. Possessing good fashion sense doesn't go unnoticed, so consider some upgrading.

Once we have attracted someone suitable, it's vital to always 100 percent respect them. They need our attention, commitment and devotion. Think about how we are offering these, and constantly up the ante.

It's very easy for couples to become bored of the same dates, which ultimately need to be more inspiring. Instead of the same old dates to familiar places shake things up by factoring in their interests to inspire ideas, which will prevent the romance from going stale.

The best approach is to put ourselves into their shoes and consider what would be an incredible date. Activities where there's physical

## Chapter 18 | How To Keep Romance Alive

touch — such as dancing, swimming or ten-pin bowling — can bring intimacy to get the sparks flying.

On the subject of looking at the relationship from their point of view, consider that when you meet up what are you expected to wear and smell like then dress according to how the date is anticipating us.

Don't be shy to introduce romantic gestures and edgy dates to try to keep a love interest's heart pumping. These will ensure that those powerful feelings last and the relationship can continue to blossom.

A well-crafted good morning and goodnight message, just explaining why we feel so in love with this special person, will always be welcomed. Who wouldn't be delighted that you care enough to think about them first thing in the morning and last thing at night? If this can be continued out of love and devotion, not as a chore or task, these loving words should put a partner in a constantly good mood.

We all love to be loved. Our someone special needs to be told how wonderful they are from time to time. Start letting the person who captured our heart know exactly how much they are adored.

A thoughtful gift every now and again will bring a smile to their face, which is so richly rewarding for both parties. Don't offer gifts every time, otherwise we are building up high expectations and this romantic gesture will be diluted.

Being attentive is essential to make love matter, and will be welcomed. Showing our romantic side, and trying to ensure we try to make our partner even happier with us, will keep the loving relationship ticking along.

## Chapter 18 | How To Keep Romance Alive

For those seeking a feel-good fix, we can far too often be fooled by the neurotransmitters of dopamine and serotonin to fall under the spell of lust instead of love.

When that occurs, the relationship is likely to fall apart. This is when the rose-tinted glasses slip off and any character flaws become apparent.

Numerous brain chemicals provide the feeling of attachment and romance, especially oxytocin — the one and only love hormone.

When we seek the perfect partner forever, we should aim to find that someone special who makes us truly happy because of the oxytocin chemicals that are released.

Oxytocin can be enhanced by caring and thoughtful actions. This can include cuddling, holding hands, sharing meals together and even watching romantic films as a couple.

Males are fortunate to determine whether their partner is 'the one' quite easily. This is because males only release oxytocin when they are with someone that they truly care about, which is what helps to create a monogamous bond.

By showing attention, care, consideration and respect towards each other you possess the main ingredients for a long-lasting and loving partnership.

Building up a natural strong bonding through simple actions and caring behavior is an investment that pays dividends to provide a meaningful romantic relationship that can ultimately last forever.

# Chapter 19 | Importance Of Intimacy

In a meaningful romantic relationship there's the need for intimacy, although there will be different levels and types of intimacy as we are all individuals with varying circumstances.

Naturally we all yearn for affection and love, with the all-important factor of physical chemistry required once our romance begins to blossom.

The physical intimacy of cuddling, hand-holding, hugging, kissing, massaging and sex are frequently part and parcel of loving relationships — especially in the early stages of a romance.

Despite the happiness that derives from this physical chemistry, relationships require superior intimacy to sustain a long-term — maybe forever — future. Key to a happy future is ensuring that there's emotional intimacy, intellectual intimacy, physical intimacy, social intimacy and spiritual intimacy.

Once the proverbial rose-tinted glasses fall off, there's a high chance of disenchantment appearing from at least one partner in a

# Chapter 19 | Importance Of Intimacy

romance. Whenever there's not the same level of commitment and devotion between two people, the relationship will ultimately come crashing down.

In stark contrast solid couples can survive and revel when their 'honeymoon' period is over through strong communication, mutual trust and support. Those partners who aren't afraid to reveal their aspirations, dreams, emotions, past romantic experiences and perspectives on life can build up a very powerful form of intimacy.

If the romance is going to last the course, any vulnerabilities will be mentally noted as the couple develop their relationship emotionally, mentally, physically and spiritually. When there's mutual commitment, connection and understanding the partnership can organically move towards sexual intimacy.

Sex can play a key role in strengthening a romantic relationship. It offers the ability to build up love and trust through the strong emotional and physical connection that has been evolving.

Although feelings of love are often present during sexual interactions, intimacy isn't just about sex. Hugs, touching and verbal communication between couples can genuinely generate feelings of emotional connection.

Emotional intimacy bodes well for meaningful relationships. Emotionally-connected couples can become well-equipped to handle any conflicts, havoc or stress within their romance. This ultimately leads to relationship longevity and possibly completes the journey for finding the perfect partner forever.

# Chapter 19 | Importance Of Intimacy

The starting point when trying to find a fulfilling romantic relationship often begins by hitting the panic button, which includes a desperate bid to find love via dating apps/websites. Offering such easy accessibility, this avenue tends to be the initial option as it's seemingly effortless at the start before it snowballs into too much communication and becomes extremely time-consuming.

The realistic prospect of finding a caring relationship online is low, unless settling for virtually anyone or being completely desperate applies.

A massive red flag is if a digital date sexualizes conversations, which indicates a one-track mind. We don't want to be lined up as their latest conquest then tossed aside. There's a huge difference between love and lust, which should never be forgotten.

Digital dating can at least deliver a swift confidence boost on a short-term basis, but after a while it can dent self-esteem. When the time comes we should follow the signal to steer ourselves towards face-to-face encounters rather than online.

If someone appears too good to be true then that's probably the case. Undertaking some online research can pay dividends and potentially lead to a proper date in the flesh.

By meeting in person there's the chance to enter conversations and check whether there's any genuine connection. It doesn't need to be love at first sight, so dating face-to-face should not be about instant chemistry and sparks flying. That sort of scenario is much more applicable to the movies than reality.

Going on dates — aside from the time, cost and rejection factors

## Chapter 19 | Importance Of Intimacy

— can fine-tune our flirting skills and hone our emotional intelligence.

This simple process will assist in the management of emotions in ourselves and others, as well as evaluate and offer the perception of whether or not we are really ready for a long-term commitment.

However, we must watch out for dates who will never be able to offer real intimacy, because we don't wish to waste our time. There are a plethora of warning signals which scream that someone's not ready for love, and that they are just after a non-committal love affair. These include being unable to cut ties to a previous relationship, a string of failed romances, constantly getting jealous and the big one of being emotionally damaged.

It's important to pay attention to actions and words during the early stages of a new relationship, both ours and our love interest, because building up intimacy is a slow-burner.

When in a budding romantic relationship we need to be wary that our latest partner isn't playing a game with our emotions. There's a huge difference between playing games and seduction.

By ignoring any early warning signs as the romance blossoms brings potential dangers, and could become extremely tricky to deal with later on. Problems should always be dealt with at the time, rather than brushed aside, by attempting to eradicate any issues through good communication.

Love making, rather than sex, is a vital cog in a romantic long-term relationship. This factor can be overlooked, and the physical intimacy of sex is just expected by many people when dating.

## Chapter 19 | Importance Of Intimacy

Yet love making greatly differs from sex. This is when the partners deeply care for each other with a fortress of affection and emotional connection. Sexual encounters, especially in the world of dating, tend to be simply fun and frolics for a short-term and meaningless partnership with no commitment.

Those eager to push and settle for a short relationship are doing so for their own selfish reasons, and tend to be like bees seeking pollen. This type of singleton will relentlessly move from one relationship to another, with their short-term partner treated like a sex object rather than someone with feelings.

Any form of true love isn't based on this sort of attitude and actions. Love may not always be the easiest thing to unearth, but mutual respect is definitely required to make a partnership work.

When it comes to respect, once couples move on from the initial stage of loving each other affectionately and developing their romantic love then love making can be introduced.

When it comes down to bedroom fun, if ever our partner becomes dissatisfied with our body then this is cause for alarm bells. The deep-rooted reality is that if our body doesn't measure up, our partner is probably used to regularly watching adult content.

If this unacceptable behavior and rejection ever occurs, which is unhealthy for our emotional well-being and self-esteem, we should immediately walk away from being truly unloved.

Love making is vital for a romantic long-term relationship to stand the test of time. Yet when we have found that seemingly elusive

## Chapter 19 | Importance Of Intimacy

perfect partner, there's going to be a time when sexual intimacy takes an unexpected dive.

Passionate intimacy — in other words the physical attraction, romance and sexual consummation — may benefit from natural aphrodisiacs.

Readily-available dietary supplement aphrodisiacs, which are designed to improve libido rather than enhance performance, could be an option. Before splashing the cash we should always consider diet and lifestyle changes, to see if things can be improved.

Well-known aphrodisiacs such as avocados, blueberries, broccoli, Champagne, cocoa, coffee, crab, extra virgin olive oil, figs, milk, oranges, oysters, red wine and salmon can work wonders.

Natural aphrodisiacs can all be a terrific energy booster and offer various other benefits. There are plenty of advantages in eating fruit and vegetables — including legumes, nuts and seafood — as well as regularly drizzling food with extra virgin oil.

Okra, a natural relaxant, helps to maintain pleasure organs. Pomegranate, by being high in oxidants, increases both romantic drive and testosterone levels. Strawberries boost romantic desire, while watermelon improves blood circulation to increase the desire for romantic love. Bananas offer bedroom stamina. Nuts — especially almonds, pistachios and walnuts — help the body to produce nitric oxide, which dilates blood vessels.

It's essential to evaluate current diets and lifestyles, keeping a record of which foods and drinks work best. After a month it's highly

# Chapter 19 | Importance Of Intimacy

probable that our mojo has resurfaced.

A quick-fix, should our lack of romantic drive still be causing stress, is to try eating dates and pure chocolate. Alternatively, we can opt for a solution of an off-the-shelf dietary supplement aphrodisiac.

More subtle and basic ways to cause an arousing effect include introducing uplifting and familiar smells, such as arousal-enhancing sweets scents of black licorice and peppermints or making fresh popcorn.

It's essential to address any ongoing issue if passionate intimacy is no longer there. It doesn't matter how many traditional remedies are tried, there needs to be the arousal and romantic desires to rekindle sexual intimacy.

Sexual intercourse is just one way that couples can express their love. It satisfies our own needs as well as the needs of our partner. It's a beautiful act of genuine caring love, respect and trust.

Once romantic desire has returned, for those in new relationships it's time to again start learning how to really respect each other and not simply go through the motions of a romantic encounter.

Should these solutions prove ineffective, opening up the channels of communication to determine whether we've reached the end of the road romantically needs to be ascertained.

A swift check is whether the relationship remains fulfilling and meaningful. To move forwards couples require the trio of must-have ingredients from the triangular theory of love — namely commitment, intimacy and passion.

Long-term commitment is about maintaining the love that's been

# Chapter 19 | Importance Of Intimacy

built up over time, while also improving it with some fine-tuning.

We should always strive to constantly strengthen our intimacy levels to feel more connected and trusting towards people and any potential partner, which lifts our physical and psychological well-being.

Generating strong feelings of closeness and connection through intimacy helps to enhance our bonding in a romantic relationship.

Those seeking their perfect forever partner should seize the day and venture to find adventure, because feeling loved is healthy for our emotional well-being and self-esteem.

We aren't programmed to be alone forever, so have an in-built urge to feel special and loved. Ensuring that we display various forms of intimacy will only improve our life and our love life.

# Chapter 20 | Happy Ever After

Just because we are feeling lonely, and want an injection of romance, are not good enough reasons to hunt down someone special to become our perfect partner forever.

As long as we tackle our quest for long-term love with realistic expectations, and accept that not every person's dream is to get married or be in a long-lasting romantic relationship, then it's time to start creating opportunities to meet someone suitable.

Finding a life partner is a major commitment. Those who have previously been married tend to be wary of walking up the aisle again, as they may have been emotionally hurt and/or financially stung by their divorce.

We don't need to feel intimidated out there scouring for our perfect partner. Cupid's arrow can strike at any time, especially when we are least expecting it. However, we should be prepared for it by constantly creating the best version of ourselves, so that someone can potentially love us.

# Chapter 20 | Happy Ever After

Naturally exuding confidence and high self-esteem will help make us appear even more attractive, and therefore highly approachable by suitable singletons.

When we do eventually find true love with that someone special, who can truly make us feel happy, it will have been worth the wait. Yet it would be a mistake to ever tell our perfect partner that all we need is love.

By seeking our perfect partner, we must know what we desire rather than concentrate on what characteristics, looks and traits we aim to avoid. Bear in mind that our ideal partner is most likely to be a mirror version of us and boasts some common interests.

Before we can fast forward to living happily ever after, we need to find this ideal person who could eventually complete our life and deliver immense happiness forever. Yet building a new and solid relationship can only occur when we are emotionally ready.

It's imperative to consider what we are really looking for romantically on a long-term basis, yet more importantly we need to appreciate what we actually can offer. Both of these appraisals will increase our confidence and make us feel comfortable, which means that any dates should run smoothly.

What prevents many singletons from finding a fulfilling romantic relationship is the fact that they still possess an aching heart. We can only move forward towards a romance when we feel ready. Otherwise we will toy with a relationship, which will probably be doomed before it has even started because our heart won't be fully committed.

# Chapter 20 | Happy Ever After

It's far better to be patient until we are ready to bounce back onto the dating scene, because then we will exude happiness that will ultimately attract people towards us. A good litmus test, so that we can happily move forwards, is to only date when we know that the next date is a possible upgrade to our previous love interest.

We all have the desire to be in an exciting relationship, which reignites our faith in romance. Unearthing a potential partner worthy of our love and devotion is not an easy task. We should wait to find someone with a common denominator and the same long-term romantic ambitions, as these factors are likely to lead to long-term happiness as a couple.

Change is the only constant in our ever-evolving lives, which we should embrace with joy. Once ready to commit to a long-term relationship we need to be selective in our process, but it's important to think outside the superficial box of just good looks and financial security. Common interests and similar character are two essential aspects, especially as looks fade over time but character does not.

Some relationships run like clockwork, and are perfect, when couples don't spend so much time together. This is when partners are happy in their own comfort zones and routines, so embrace their part-time independence.

When emotionally available potential partners are our equal in terms of background, interests and looks, these ingredients are a recipe for success. Yet to maintain happiness in a long-term relationship there must be amazing connection and remarkable intimacy.

## Chapter 20 | Happy Ever After

Finding someone to settle down with is a big commitment, especially if both parties previously suffered unsatisfying relationships for whatever reasons. That fear factor is an important hurdle to overcome for some to commit to a long-term romance.

Having the unequivocal desire to find the love of our life, and a soulmate, once entering a new relationship can be a very idealized love. If partners agree to move things along at a pace to suit them both, and there's no problems when the 'honeymoon' period is over, then this is a step in the right direction on the journey to long-term happiness.

We all crave to unearth someone who loves and respects us, ideally finding a romantic relationship where there are zero doubts. That means overcoming differences of opinion and problems, which will have most likely been caused by frustration, as a formidable dream team.

The right sort of arguing can actually be healthy for a relationship. It shows that we care and are passionate enough to fight. As long as a couple makes progress when arguing, as opposed to each individual trying to win the fight, everything is going in the right direction for a fulfilling long-term future.

Sprinklings of sincerity and understanding are vital elements to helping create the perfect dish of love. To cook up a long-lasting romantic relationship on the menu, it needs to have plenty of the right ingredients such as empathy, loyalty, strong communication and trust.

# Chapter 20 | Happy Ever After

Couples who find long-term happiness ensure that both have the same relationship, in other words there isn't one who gives more than the other otherwise this would comprise two individuals striving for different aspirations and goals.

Forming a truly loving relationship is all about what will work for both parties and their vision for the future. However, for a full-on relationship it's time to appreciate that we have to compromise, show empathy and build up mutual respect to be fully compatible.

Molding ourselves to form a solid partnership is never going to be simplistic. As we get older this becomes much more difficult, because singletons often find themselves set in their ways. Those who have been divorced or widowed will arguably embrace being able to do what they want, and when they want, without having to consider their nearest and dearest.

For a happy romantic relationship to work, it's best to be crystal clear from the start about anything that makes us feel uncomfortable. Communicating concerns is acceptable, and if there's mutual respect any changes will be automatic. This approach is recommended to successfully maintain a solid relationship, because when there's genuine love we should be happy to compromise and make the necessary changes.

We aren't supposed to love everything about our partner, so if there's something one party doesn't like we should try to change it after explaining why.

Poor communication between couples is the biggest killer of

# Chapter 20 | Happy Ever After

romantic relationships, so it's best to always address any difficulties to keep the partnership nicely ticking along.

As much as we often try to hang onto a relationship that's fading, refusing to admit to ourselves that our partner wasn't committed on a long-term basis, we can let things drift on for an easy life.

There's not always the wonderful living happily ever after scenario for most couples, as they aren't committed when things aren't perfect because they only want fun and frolics.

Our personal growth as a couple needs to be encouraged and supported by each party in order for a forever relationship to truly work.

Getting our partner involved in conversation, jolting their mind about memories created together and arranging exciting plans for happy times as a couple are ways to both focus on the future. Happiness is when our partner utters those special three words of "I love you" for a good reason, which can give us goosebumps and melt our heart.

These moments will help build up a loving relationship, rather than be complacent and let it fall flat, because it is all about the combined happiness generated.

If we are ever unsure about where our romance is going, it's worth suggesting a repeat of a magical moment next year as it was loved so much. By exploring the future we should be able to establish where we stand in their mind, and on a long-term basis, without being too direct and impolite.

What deeply motivates us to create a happy future together is

## Chapter 20 | Happy Ever After

having a purpose in life. Romantic relationships require some purpose and direction. Yet both parties must show the desire and inclination to make it work. With exciting plans in place, partnerships can develop into loving, long-term relationships with just a few tweaks.

When both parties are caring, giving, kind and thoughtful these actions help to cement the love and trust. It takes two to determine what is truly wanted out of a romantic relationship. For longevity we should ideally have similar morals, values and ways of thinking.

Keeping intimacy alive and showing empathy maintains the love, which reiterates why our partner permanently has a special place in our heart and soul.

We may encounter a number of bumps on the road to long-term happiness, yet the best loving partners are those who actually want to be in a romantic relationship for the right reasons.

Happiness is a choice, and we should pick it. That special someone that we want to spend forever with will gradually know us intimately for many years to come. This is the person who is determined to make us happy by sharing both the good times and bad times.

Forever happiness in a loving relationship is truly attainable by appreciating what we have and being grateful for the partner we picked.

By opting to be with someone special forever is a life-changer, and having the desire to make a loving relationship last the course helps us develop into a much better and happier individual.

Although no one is perfect, and the fact that it's virtually impossible to love everything about a potential partner, when it comes to love

# Chapter 20 | Happy Ever After

we must take the rough with the smooth to share disappointments and sheer happiness.

What's essential is to ensure that our special someone really does make us so happy, by constantly bringing a smile to our face, that we would like this perfect partner and wonderful feeling of love to last a lifetime.

Milton Keynes UK
Ingram Content Group UK Ltd.
UKHW041204051024
449185UK00004B/23